The Pop Process

The *POP* Process

Richard Mabey

 Hutchinson Educational

HUTCHINSON EDUCATIONAL LTD
178–202 Great Portland Street, London W1

London Melbourne Sydney
Auckland Bombay Toronto
Johannesburg New York

First published 1969

*This book has been set in Imprint, printed in Great Britain
on Antique Wove paper, and bound by The Camelot Press Ltd
London and Southampton*

09 098870 1

Contents

Acknowledgements

For permission to reprint copyright material the author is indebted to the following:

Encounter for an extract from 'A Map of the Underground' by Peter Fryer (October, 1967); *Evening Standard* and Miss Maureen Cleave for an extract from 'The Year Pop Went Flat' (29 December, 1966); Adrian Mitchell and Odham's Press for an extract from a review in *Woman's Mirror*; *New Society* for extracts from articles by Colin Fletcher (20 February, 1964), Benedict Nightingale (5 October, 1967), Patterson (15 September, 1966) and Reyner Banham (1 December, 1966); *New Statesman* for extracts from articles by Wilfred Mellers (24 February, 1967, and 2 June, 1967); the *Observer* for extracts from an article by John Crosby (7 May, 1967); *Peace News* for extracts from an article by David Horowitz (11 December, 1964); the *Spectator* for extracts from articles by Mario Amaya (14 July, 1967) and Kenneth Allsop (9 December, 1966).

Preface

Writing a book about the pop scene is like making a will. Every new shift of fashion means another inky revision, another old friend deleted. There's no real hope of ever catching up. So I fear that those readers who come to this book for the latest news from the pop front will be disappointed. Nor will there be much in it that is new to enthusiasts who have had their ears close to the scene for the last half-dozen years. It is not that sort of book at all—which is why I think that, when all is said and done, the dating problem is not a serious one.

I wrote *The Pop Process* principally for curious adults—parents, teachers, youth leaders—who, whilst not being antagonistic to pop music, are perplexed about the role it has come to play in young people's lives, and indeed in our society as a whole. My aim has been to look at the function and meaning of the scene, and only secondarily at this or that temporal instance. So the sections of the book (all of which are dated) are more 'patches' of history than sequences in a historical documentary. Even the style of the writing, I noticed with some amusement whilst reading the proofs, reflects the multitude of moods which pop has assumed during the past decade.

Much has happened in the pop world since the manuscript went to press, notably the continuing development of 'progressive' pop, represented at its richest and most exciting in American groups like Country Joe and the Fish and the Mothers of Invention. But, as I said above, one has to call a halt some-where. I do so without too troubled a conscience though, as I believe that the analysis of the function of the scene presented here still applies to what is happening now.

An enormous number of people have helped in some way in the preparation of this book. I owe a special dept of gratitude to all the young people who are, in a sense, the raw material of this book: to my old students who answered my queries with such long-suffering patience; to the girls who endured my dance-floor writhings; and to the many more anonymous ones who did not object to my stares.

Without Richard Simon's encouragement the first draft of this book would have been consigned to the fire. My heartfelt thanks to him and the many other friends who read and com-mented so wisely on different parts and drafts: Kenneth Allsop, Jeff Cloves, Jackie Haslam, Peter Newmark, Michael Schofield, Paddy Whannel, and especially my brother David, whose encyclopaedic knowledge and visionary understanding of con-temporary pop were a source of continuing sustenance.

RICHARD MABEY

May, 1969

Part One

1 Introduction*

As long ago as 1958, that wise social critic, Colin MacInnes, wrote these words about pop music:

> I'd like to say that I think the abysmal ignorance of educated persons about the popular music of the millions is deplorable. First, because pop music, on its own level, can be so good; and I have never met anyone who, condemning it completely, has turned out on close enquiry to know anything whatever about it. But worse, because the deaf ear that's turned in pained disdain away from pop music betrays a lamentable lack of curiosity about the culture of our country in 1958. For that music *is* our culture: at all events the anthropologist from Sao Paulo or Peking would esteem it so, and rightly. Alfred Deller, yes; but what about Lonnie Donegan, he'd say? They're both of our world, and there's no doubt which of these two siren voices penetrates and moulds more English hearts and brains.[1]

It has taken nearly ten years for this advice to be heeded, and for pop to be lifted out of the gossip and show-biz columns and given regular analytical and critical consideration.

The Beatles, of course, must take most of the credit for breaking the intellectuals' boycott of popular music. The phenomenon of their initial success marked something of a real turning-point in attitudes towards pop. A group who sang with Merseyside accents, who were obviously more amused than impressed by their success and who brought to Tin Pan Alley the rare virtues of honesty and enthusiasm, could not be

* February, 1968.

[1] *Twentieth Century*, February, 1958.

explained according to the old formulas. Nor could the subsequent discovery that Liverpool housed over four hundred other professional beat groups. But the interest began to die as soon as the phenomenon lost its novelty, and it has only been sustained and built upon because of the constant diffusion of interest and attention from areas which are not strictly anything to do with pop music. One thinks immediately of the Mod/Rocker troubles, the drug scares, and the extraordinary involvement, in 1967, of hard-headed extrovert beat groups with introspective Eastern mysticism. Events like these were essentially by-products, side- (if not freak-) shows outside the main carnival. But they gathered in—indeed they demanded—sympathetic and intelligent eyes, that quickly came to focus in addition on related developments in the mainstream of pop. As always, behind every pathological outburst were discovered marks of real social and cultural development: here an increase of tolerance, there a broadening of the definitions of what pop music was capable of communicating.

The few stalwarts who in the early 'sixties could be relied upon to write sympathetically about the pop scene—MacInnes, Adrian Mitchell, Kenneth Allsop, George Melly—now have counterparts in sanctums as august as the *Listener* and *The Times*. Most critics, in fact, with the dexterity with which that profession seems to have recently credited itself, have begun to take occasional, dissective looks at the pop scene, as it encroaches in one direction on the theatre and in the other on classical music. There is, no doubt, some Hawthorne Effect at work here, for pop is a new and fashionable intellectual property. But underneath I think one can sense a growing conviction that Colin MacInnes was right: that like it yet or not, this *is* our culture. At the very least it seems, in artists like Bob Dylan and the Beatles, to have potentialities for growth that justify a close and affectionate scrutiny.

But if we are a long way past the stage of blaming pop music for every conceivable teenage vice and attempting to evaluate it, when we bothered at all, by the criteria of literary criticism, we are not much closer to understanding the fundamental nature of the pop scene. Topical, journalistic coverage can of necessity only sketch in momentary and ephemeral outlines. We can catch glimpses through these of a broader pattern at work, but its real meaning and mode of operation are still largely a mystery. It is not clear even now, for instance, what pop music really *is*, or how it works, or how new fashions are generated.

There is, of course, one major reason why such a study in depth has not yet emerged, and that is the rapid obsolescence of the case material. It's impossible to discuss pop without looking at the specifics and naming the names. Yet as little as six months after such a commitment has been made the inexorable march of fashion may have caused your example to be forgotten, invalidated the significance you attached to it, and even challenged your priorities in choosing to discuss it at all.

I should perhaps come clean at this point and explain that *The Pop Process* is an attempt to surmount this problem. The rationale behind its structure is this: if you cannot avoid the problems of dating, make use of them. I have taken the position that there is an argument for an honest admission of the way in which once-valued examples may decay, and even for an exposure, a museum show, if you like, of the fact that this has happened. Such a process is, after all, living evidence of pop's metabolism.

The body of this book was written in the winter of 1965, as the flurry of Merseybeat was dying down and pop was entering one of its periodic recessions. It is an attempt to examine the nature of the pop scene by looking at the dominant role of fashion, and the ways in which new styles are generated. Many of its interpretations do, I think, still hold good today. But inevitably certain examples have passed into oblivion, certain explanations have been shown to be naïve in the light of what has happened since, and certain preoccupations proved to be misplaced. Wherever this has happened (provided the judgements seemed to be not too far removed from those which were being generally made in 1965) I have, as a deliberate part of the philosophy behind the book, left them as they were written.

Against them are juxtaposed reprints of articles about

developments in pop during the two succeeding years. These I hope will work as snapshots, fossil records of the evolution of the pop landscape between 1965 and 1967. Like fossils, their messages about extinct forms only tell their full story in the context of the continuing development of the organism.

What overall conclusions about the working of the scene has this counterpoint brought into focus? First, that the rough model of the operation of the scene presented as the main body of this text seems to have held good for subsequent fashions. The hippy phase, for instance, for all its extravagances and cotton-wool philosophies, conformed precisely to the standard pattern of grass-roots origins, rapid diffusion, band-waggoning, exploitation, and auto-destruction.

On a more specific level, the popularity of the blues continued to grow, lyrics improved (though not without venturing down some embarrassingly blind alleys) and the Beatles broke quite new ground. Engelbert Humperdinck proved the inherent diversity of the scene by becoming the housewife's choice during the Indian summer of '67, and Radio One bounced on to the air with a waxwork imitation of the pirates, 'absolutely lifelike but clearly lifeless', as George Melly put it.

Bob Dylan, though, was vindicated, and the widespread unhappiness with his change of style which is noted in a later chapter proved to be one of the wilder misunderstandings of 1965. It took, as we shall see, the publicly-flaunted dogmatism of the British folk audience, the fake lyricism of flower music and two years of hard listening to show just how good the new Dylan was. The resentment against his change in direction turned out to be as much a result of his involvement with the scene as was the change itself.

Scene changes

But there has been one major shift which has overshadowed all these rearrangements of detail. The real focus of interest, the storm centre of pop, has been transferred from the 'scene' to the music itself: for 'teenagers' and 'idols' you will now read 'audience' and 'performers'. This is not, of course, to say that social considerations are irrelevant. The scene still plays a therapeutic role for teenagers, fashions still change in the same rhythmic pattern, and a few groups, like the Monkees and Dave Dee *et alia*, continue to fulfil the idolatrous needs of 12- to 14-year-old fans.

But it is no longer sufficient to discuss pop *purely* in terms of its social significance, because it now has, in addition, a quite definable artistic role. This is not because the music is uniformly better, though much of it is; nor because more of the audience are listening, which they are (but this is not a useful criterion for judging the quality of a popular form). It is simply that pop music has at last become aware of itself. While it continued to be a purely functional form, used by the audience as a supermarket for emotional pep-ups and identity symbols, and played by the groups for complementary reasons, any analysis had in its turn to be primarily a functional one. Now writers, singers, and record-producers are self-consciously theorizing about their music. We are seeing in fact the evolution of the jack-of-all-trades popster. Poet, musician, actor, cracker-barrel mystic and businessman, he is beginning to articulate, however primitively, the relation of his art to, say, sport and advertising, and to borrow ideas and stances from other media and cultures.

We can see this overall change of emphasis echoed and partially explained in half-a-dozen different ways. Only a few years ago it would have been realistic to say that any new idea in pop had been stolen from the jazz or blues tradition.[1] Now we are in a situation where pop musicians are working from proto-types in their own genre. You will hear groups described as playing in the 'West Coast style', and guitarists modelling themselves on Eric Clapton or Jimi Hendrix. That this reverent emulation may be a piece of unhistorical self-deception—Clapton himself, for instance, has simply alchemized the style

[1] The flow in the opposite direction, from pop to jazz, remains un-checked. Jazz bands, whether trad or progressive, have always used pop standards as the raw material for their improvisations. The increased melodic and harmonic subtleties of contemporary pop have merely give the jazzmen more to work on.

of coloured urban blues originals like Albert King—does not matter; 'master and apprentice' is the way the tyro sees the situation.

Much of this is due to a proliferation of brilliant—though often musically illiterate and self-taught—instrumentalists: Mike Bloomfield, Eric Clapton and Jeff Beck on guitar; Ginger Baker on drums; Alan Price and Al Kooper on organ; and Stevie Winwood, multi-talented eighteen-year-old prodigy of just about every pop instrument. All are products of the countless small beat groups that burgeoned during the early 'sixties, whose ruthless apprenticeship schemes involved instant, corrective feedback, every night, from hundreds of querulous teenagers. It was an impeccable training in the fine arts of timing and swing.

There has been borrowing, too, from other musical traditions, most obviously from India. George Harrison learned the sitar to some effect under Ravi Shankar, and the latter returned the compliment by playing before thousands of hippies at the 1967 Monterey pop festival. Many songs, in fact, showed evidence of Eastern influences, though in most cases this consisted of no more than a music-box, quarter-tone embellishment grafted on to the end of solidly Western choruses.

But India was only one of many sources. The Rolling Stones went back to baroque for *Lady Jane*, and the Beatles to George Formby and the Music Hall for *When I'm Sixty Four*. Hurdy-gurdies, harpsichords, string quartets and whole symphony orchestras were heard amongst the backing sounds of the more progressive groups.

Unfortunately, this authentic re-working has set a precedent, and opened up a short cut to facile originality. But in another way its example may prove to be of inestimable value to pop music. Borrowing and blending are the traditional chemical processes by which all new popular forms originate. We should have no jazz (in its broadest sense) at all if it was not for the happy coincidence in New Orleans of a multitude of different musical traditions: French light orchestral music, Civil War marches, Negro blues, White Baptist hymns, and Cuban dance-music.

A great deal of this miscegenation has taken place in a quite new institution (for the pop world)—the music workshop. This is more grandiose in name than in practice, where it often means no more than a commitment by one group to a period of private experiment. Implied always in such a retreat is a need to escape from the distorting pressures of the scene, which, as hinted at later, are stifling to any sort of creativity. Nirvana, two of whose members are graduates of the Royal Academy of Music, have, at the time of writing, only given one live concert. The audience's bewilderment at their performance convinced them that they should concentrate on the music workshop idea, developing new material in private for sit-down concerts and records only. Traffic, led by ex-Spencer-Davis wonder-boy, Stevie Winwood, sought extremes of isolation. Its four members locked themselves away for six months in a tumble-down cottage in the heart of the Berkshire countryside.

This desire to opt out of the frenetic world of one-night stands, hysterical audiences and inevitably shoddy stage performances is being demonstrated by a growing number of groups. Both the Stones and the Beatles have declared that they are unlikely to give any more live performances. (They have also taken over their own managerships, thereby setting adrift even further the exploitation theory of pop.) Bryan Wilson of the Beach Boys and Pete Townshend of the Who have even built recording studios in their homes.

We can see this lack of interest in live performances reflected in other changes in the scene: the run-down of fan clubs, for instance, and the low temperature of airport receptions. The last riot I saw (at Heathrow, for the Monkees) was precipitated as much by children as teenagers.

The idol—the creature of the public—is being supplanted by the musician, who is very much his own man. So the public stage show gives way to the private recording studio, and questions in the pop press about singers' favourite foods become investigations of the philosophical implications of their lyrics.

The transfer of interest from the singer as personality to the singer as performer has been accelerated in one direction by the disembodied attributes he has acquired on disc. It is a common misunderstanding, outside the pop industry, to suppose that records and live performances are substitutes for one another; that, for instance, a group are inadequate musicians if they cannot duplicate the elaborate and sophisticated sound of their records in a club. The cinema once made the same mistake, and began its career by attempting to reproduce theatrical performances on film.

But records like the Beatles' *Sgt Pepper's Lonely Hearts Club Band* have made it abundantly clear that the elaborate electronic syntheses of the recording studio are an artistic process in their own right, and are not simply ways of disguising poor musicianship. Experts like George Martin, who supervises the Beatles' recordings, are men of considerable musical talents. They have under their control equipment that can reproduce electronically almost any imagined sound. They can add to a voice: echo, vibrato, fuzz, or phasing (an effect similar to the drifting out of tune of a distant radio station), delete its bass frequencies altogether (as in *Day in the Life*), blend in separately-recorded string orchestras and choirs, make one guitar sound like a siren and another as if it is being played with a fluttering trumpet mute. When the separate recordings of the different instruments and voices have been completed (usually on parallel tracks on one multi-track tape), the recording supervisor and the artists will together choose the best takes and splice them into a finished master tape. (This of course is also standard practice in concert music recording.) There are tricks which can be added even at this late stage. Loops of a constantly repeated phrase can be incorporated, and snatches of music spliced in backwards as in *Strawberry Fields Forever*.

Sgt Pepper took six months and several hundreds of hours in the studios to produce. Compare this with the first fifty-minute L.P. of a live performance specialist, Jimi Hendrix, which was reputedly put together in just over one hour!

This laboratory manufacture of what some regard as *ersatz* music is still foreign to our conception of the way in which 'art' should be created. Looking at the unidirectional mikes, the musicians' padded headphones, and the recording manager behind his soundproof glass panel, we miss the quick, feeling relationship between artist and audience on which our traditional notions of popular art are based. But this is our prejudice, not a comment on the quality of the product, as a look at the status of any good professional photographer will testify. For all their telephoto lenses and negative bleaching baths these are now accepted as thorough-going artists. All equipment does is to give the artist greater scope for translating his visions and fantasies into reality. The choice of vision still has to be made, the humanity of the music preserved.

The only real mischief to be found in all this is that the efforts of gifted recording managers and professional sessions musicians are often attributed, for selling purposes, to teenage stars who had little or nothing to do with the making of a record. A notorious example of this was the Love Affair's Number One hit in January 1968, *Everlasting Love*. Immediately this had left its position at the top, the group confessed that only one of its five members actually played on the record; the others 'couldn't learn it in time'.[1]

The phylogenesis of this new category of music and the developing repertoire of pure recorded sound, has forced a sort of natural selection on the live-performance tradition. Those groups that relied upon the imitation of recorded music have been very largely weeded out (except from small provincial clubs, where good dance music is all that is required). In their place have evolved groups with a much more physical and *dramatic* appeal (in the theatrical sense). This is separate from the 'lonely boy' act and embarrassingly contrived hip-shaking

[1] This incident speeded through the Musician's Union's charter against ghosting, and precipitated this astonishing letter in the music press.

I am not a pop fan but the mother of Lynton Guest, organist and pianist with the Love affair. I should like to make it clear that my son can read and play music.

He has certificates of distinction from the Royal Schools of Music for playing, sight reading and theory, also first awards from the Leicester Competitive Festival of Music.

He joined the pop world against my wishes because he loves every moment. Otherwise he would have gone into another field of music. *Melody Maker*, 2 March, 1968.

of the early rock'n'roll performers, and even further from the 'shows' of combos like the Barron Knights with their impersonations and signature tunes.

This is not to say, though, that the developing dramatic tradition in pop is entirely original. Indeed, it is borrowing very heavily from the ideas associated with Happenings and spontaneous theatre. The Herd have thrown bananas to their audiences (and had them thrown back), the Creation have painted pictures, the Move destroyed cars and television sets, and Arthur Brown (of the Crazy World of Arthur Brown) has set fire to himself. The Who made for a while a philosophy out of destroying their instruments and found that Americans 'brought up in an incredibly materialistic society . . . just couldn't believe that anyone would deliberately destroy anything worth money'.

Most of the groups' antics lack this ideological groundbase, and are, finally, artless and tedious. But they do imply a recognition of the separateness of live and recorded music, and of the essential physicality of the former.

But the most significantly physical live performer of all, Jimi Hendrix, uses no artifices at all during the main body of his act. When his first record, *Hey Joe*, appeared, it seemed as if the only remarkable things about him were his prodigious guitar technique and his tender age. Then his shattering and blatantly sensous act was seen.

Hendrix has achieved that rare fusion between instrument and player that inspired the Spanish phrase for a guitarist and his instrument, 'six strings and a heart'. One journalist has described him as 'a ventriloquist of the guitar'. During a song he will play it effortlessly behind his back, pick it with his teeth, and caress it between his legs. All the time he will be producing an explosive but perfectly controlled blitz of sound from the instrument, from the disgruntled bass chattering that emerges as he vanishes, hunch-shouldered, behind the amplifiers, to the hollow reverberating whine, escalating with feedback, that has become his trademark. His whole body reinforces the sounds he produces. The curl of the lips, the rapid turn of the head, the lean, the hunch are a perfect articulation of the muscular progression of the music. I've referred later in the book to 'internalized dancing', to the way in which beat music and especially the blues demands from the listener a *physical* response. A slow-blooming, *sostenuto* top C, knifing its way from a guitar sound system working at a few hundred watts, can have the same effect as a feather brushed gradually up the spine.

Hendrix, guitar and man, is a configuration in space of the tension inherent in the music at any given point; his movements, a choreography of the audience's internalized responses. And the dynamics of his act can give us two useful clues as to the way that pop music operates. First, it suggests that patterns of muscular release and tension, associated with the changing mood of the music, could be the source of the split-second timing that is needed to generate those indefinable qualities of swing and drive. Second, that pop music communicates a great deal not only at a non-verbal level, but also at a non-musical level. Gestures, postures, movements are all meaningful in relation to the music and the lyrics.[1] They help to form a framework of known signs inside which the significance and tenor of the music can be more easily understood. So the harem neck-jerking of Reg Presley (of the Troggs) renders his threateningly sexual lyrics jokingly innocuous; and the wry, mobile mouth of Ray Davies (of the Kinks) adds an authoritative wisdom to his perceptive little ballads.

These clues to the way pop communicates non-verbally have also clarified the sort of words that *can* work in a song. Psychedelic music, as we shall see below, threw up the most embarrassingly pretentious lyrics of the decade. Much of this was due to the insincerity and ineptitude of the song-writers, who were faced for the first time in their careers with the necessity of writing fashionably about technicolour visions instead of shop-girl daydreams.

[1] Compare, for instance, our instinctive head-shake when the pleasure given by the music is 'too much' (meaning 'No, please stop') with the identical gesture in Indian music, where it is a formal signal of approval and admiration from one player to another.

But it is now clear that they also failed because the meaningful lyric is the most difficult goal to achieve in pop music. The traps are scattered like a minefield. Amongst those songs that have clearly *tried* to say something, we can see the discouraging results of over-simplification (the protest craze) over-abstraction and naïve impressionism (hippy songs); fake simplicity (songs like Traffic's *Hole in My Shoe*); over-powerful music obscuring the lyrics (most of the Rolling Stones' numbers); over-romanticized lyrics getting in the way of the music (the contemporary British folk tradition, Bert Janscht and the Incredible String Band, all brilliant instrumentalists but fond of capital letters for life and love). Add to this the temptation to over-personalize that is evident in some of Dylan's more exasperating songs, and you have a catalogue of pitfalls that covers the whole range of verbal expression.

It is clear that pop music, as a matrix, imposes strictly defined limits upon the sort of lyrics which will work. The songwriter has to steer a path between the true story and the myth, the specific and the symbolic, the personally experienced and the generally apprehended, the chant and the poem. And the conventions involved in the way that pop communicates ensure that all inappropriateness, insincerity and over-complexity are ruthlessly exposed.

Heroes lost

Most remorselessly of all is unmasked the pretentiousness of the synthetically meaningful song, the insult inherent in any attempt to manufacture ideas to a formula. The worst and most pervasive example of this practice was the fashion for flower music which bloomed during 1967.

The story of the progress of this fad illuminates in a salutary way some of the built-in weaknesses and vulnerabilities of a commercially-based popular music. In certain respects the hippies and their music were exceptional. Unlike any pop sub-culture before, they had a consciously articulated ideology, based on dropping out, 'doing your own thing', ethereal ideals of Universal Love and Beauty, and an eclectic religiosity. The manifestations of this philosophy pushed the pop scene as far as it could go this side of sanity. Clothes became a dazzling collage of Eastern silks, gipsy ornaments and astrological symbols. The music, with a curious schizoid inconsistency, veered between the very un-loving orgiastic stage violence of the Move and the Crazy World of Arthur Brown, and the flabby, muslin songs of Traffic.

But for all its excesses, Flower Power's exploitation as a fashion and its failure to contribute anything original or valuable to the musical heritage of pop, were just two more illustrations of the surprisingly constant workings of the pop scene.

Bogus diffusion and exploitation began early in the life of the fad, in spite of its genuinely popular—albeit confused— roots in the States. As *Time* reporters and weekend drop-outs wafted into San Francisco in the summer, hoping for a quick plug-in to instant revelation, the genuine hippies trudged out. A poem taped to a Haight-Ashbury shop-window expressed the situation with some acumen.

> Perhaps
> Wearing plastic flowers
> Might control
> Slow death
> If
> You could accept
> The plastic people
> Wearing them.

In this country the fashion was taken up by pop stars, followers and commercialists with only the misunderstood dregs of the philosophy that had underpinned the American movement. The springy exhilaration that had characterized the scene in 1963 collapsed into a tinted, blancmange bonhomie; the political significance which 'dropping-out' possessed in the States was ignored, and the redeeming features of West Coast music (it was, in the main, lively, progressive rock'n'roll plus intelligent social criticism) were overlooked in favour of the fairground-booth mysticism of a few rearguard groups.

The most saddening thing was the acquiescence of those four

cheeky Lancashire upstarts. Like converts at a Billy Graham convention ('every head bowed, every eye closed' described the new craze with deadly accuracy) they surrendered meekly to the Maharishi,[1] pledged themselves to Love and the Light Within, and began being polite to reporters. It was a perfect but dispiriting theatrical symbol of the whole reversal.

Interviewed about *his* new-found religious beliefs, Graham Nash of the Hollies pronounced:

> I don't believe we come from this planet. If man started from a central point, there'd be no difference among us. There'd be no coloured people, no Asians, etc. It's my belief that other planets each put their own types on Earth and are watching to see who wins out.[2]

Eric Burdon, once the most level-headed, uncompromising of British singers, learned mysticism from a London taxi driver and wrote on the cover of his L.P.: 'I love you all. . . . If you feel alone and confused and unhappy, discontented, just know that I (and there are many more like me) love you. . . .' Which was comforting for us, but not so for the American cops he derided in his record, *San Franciscan* (where else) *Nights*. Nor did the lullaby verse in the same song on the notorious Hell's Angels motor-cycle gang clarify his disturbingly contradictory attitudes.

But by then there were very few who were thinking clearly. Mick Jagger and Marianne Faithfull announced they had seen green men alight from a flying saucer. Scott Walker related in the Eamonn Andrews Show that he knew a Russian scientist who had successfully built a faster-than-light spaceship. Julie Felix, one-time protest singer and lone independent voice on Juke Box Jury, became a grinning success-predictor, and produced an L.P. called *Flowers*. And the Nite People vowed that they were told to record *Summertime Blues* by spirit voices at a séance. As Pete Quaife said mournfully of the 'love thing': 'It changed a lot of good blokes, who everybody rated, into creeps.'[3]

[1] In Los Angeles the Maharishi advertised along the lines 'for fifteen minutes and 5 dollars a day I can make you a new man'.
[2] *Disc*, 14 October, 1967.
[3] *Melody Maker*, 11 November, 1967.

But it would be as unfair to accuse these old heroes of 'selling out' as it would be to attribute their metamorphosis to the personality-corroding power of LSD. In retrospect, their rapid transformation may be seen as no more than a symptom of their final absorption of show-biz traditions. Fringe religions have always attracted entertainers too temperamental and profesionally insecure to have no faith, yet too bohemian to adopt a conventional one. It's no great surprise to see the Buddhas and prayer-beads of the new generation of troupers alongside the Tarot Cards and palmistry charts of the old.

But the unique pace-setting relationship which exists between a top-flight star and the pop scene makes his conversion a matter of much more import than the spiritualist sessions of an ageing theatrical. Flower power deadened the nerve of toughness and common sense which had been the saving grace of British pop since the subsequently infanticidal Beatles gave birth to it.

On the commercial scene its influence was all the more ludicrous because of the underlying hint of spiritual meaningfulness. Bells and kaftans blossomed in supermarkets, and bead stalls sprung up on street corners. One irreverent Asian protested that, 'You spent centuries trying to give away beads to us; now you want them back'. A teenage magazine published an article entitled 'A Raver's Guide to Transcendental Meditation'. And in June, 1967, outside a rockers' café in Hertfordshire, I saw beat-up Zephyrs with bells tied to their aerials.

Groups were pushed uneasily into togas and necklaces and advertised in awesome pre-Raphaelite poses. A group called John's Children were photographed in the nude for their poster, and only just made decent by strategic placing of the obligatory flora. Said their leader: 'The flower power scene came around us and has now left us. When the idea caught on we were more or less pushed into it. The flower bit is such a commercialized rat race now.'[1] A more unsavoury example of exploitation was unearthed by, of all people, David Jacobs. After playing, on Juke Box Jury, a love-credo by one Alexander Bell, he invited the singer to come and talk to him. Jacobs

[1] *Melody Maker*, 11 November, 1967.

suggested that the identity between the singer's surname and one of the major icons of the hippy cult was a little too convenient to explain away by coincidence. Mr Bell, who had presumably expected the usual velvet glove treatment, was dumbfounded. He refused to comment on the publicity leaflet which David Jacobs produced and which gave the singer's real name as Robin Hunt. Whereupon Jacobs revealed that the song, dramatically entitled *Alexander Bell Believes*, was in fact what two middle-aged songwriters believed.

I cannot think of one flower song that did not exhibit the same mechanical attempt to duplicate a philosophical idea. The formula was simple: take any conventional, romantic song and replace Lover's Lane with Main Drag, San Francisco, and 'heart' with 'mind'. The following lines, all from 1967 songs, could, with that one word altered, come straight from a Broadway musical: 'The sunshine will make your mind grow up to the sky'; 'I'll tell you something which will gladden your mind'; 'Listen to your mind'; 'Lose your dreams and you will lose your mind'; 'Listen in the silence of your mind'.

The whole lyrical output of the flower movement had the facile automatism of Dial-a-Prayer (reflecting the short cuts to bliss and progressive music represented by LSD and grafted-on sitars).[1] Sometimes, in true ad-agency style, childlike images (tin soldiers, wizards, toymakers) replaced the primeval mind as the symbols of innocence. In fact, Alan Bown managed to fell the two kites with one stone in the devastating line, 'We'll all go down and blow our minds in Toyland'. Even Traffic, in

[1] As indeed did many of the record reviews. The following, by Nick Jones of the *Melody Maker*, was typical:

The Nice: *The Thoughts of Emerlist Davjack*.

To believe or not to believe this was once P. P. Arnold's backing group before a monstrous cosmic explosion hurtled them on to another path, leading up tinkling, spiralling staircases where they found a together, unified kind of propulsion which put energy into their thoughts, soul into their sound, and their space was nice. This is the Nice, they are, and their first record is, and they wrote it, and played it, and produce it, and they produce enough heavenly energy for four groups, let alone for four people. But that's where the mysterious Emerlist Davjack comes in with his eternal youth and chartbusting music.

spite of their six months in seclusion, were unable to produce anything more than a random jumble of Edward Lear and Big Rock Candy Mountain images.

> *I looked in the sky and an elephant's eye*
> *Was looking at me from a bubble-gum tree.*

Nor were the Beatles entirely blameless. *Challenge*, the paper of the Young Communist Movement, was unfair to call their record *Sgt Pep-Up's Phoney Thoughts Club Band*; but it must be said that, judged on its lyrics alone, the record is an inconsistent one, and that the unpretentious, down-to-earth songs like *She's Leaving Home* and *Good Morning* are far superior to the freaky word games of *Lucy in the Sky with Diamonds* and the watery pantheism of *Within You*. (How one hopes that the Beatles, when they make their Indian pilgrimage, will visit Bihar as well as the Maharishi's palace.)

The reasons for the superior quality of their earlier lyrics were underlined in an interview Paul Macartney gave to Alan Aldridge.[1] He explained how they were based on real fragments of the group's collective experience: the half-glimpsed *Daily Mirror* headlines, the playground jokes.

And heroes found

The lesson is disarmingly simple. The authentic personal statement produces the best song lyrics in the way that it has always produced the most convincing art of every other sort.

One who has learnt this lesson is Ray Davies, writer and lead singer for the Kinks. His songs are cheeky, nostalgic and as simple and clear-cut as nursery rhymes. He has captured in words, music and sheer personal presence the timeless flavour of Hoggart's England, seaside holidays, Sunday lunch and all. His *Waterloo Sunset* is the most evocative London ballad in the whole *genre*, a veritable *Horse's Mouth* in song. *Autumn Almanac*, another atmospheric piece, was structured like an operetta:

[1] *Observer*, 26 November, 1967.

I'm working to the point where each recording would incorporate a whole show. I hate the way that, even now, you have to put in an obvious hook-phrase and then keep repeating it as many times as you can. I'd like to do songs where you'd put across an idea once and then go on to something completely different, a bit in the same way as a symphony, progressing from movement to movement and not being tied to any one phrase.[1]

The same approach is being explored by the Who, who emerged in the autumn of 1967, after several months' hibernation, with ideas about music that were in radical contradiction to those of the currently fashionable hippy movement. The L.P. which they brought out late in 1967, *The Who Sells Out*, was an ad-opera containing very contemporary fairy-story songs about people with problems which were solved by the application of branded products. The sleeve shows one of the group sitting in a hip-bath full of Heinz baked beans. (Heinz were delighted and sent them a crate of the product free.)

Pete Townshend, songwriter and intellectual of the group, explained in an interview with Nik Cohn why he wanted to write songs of this sort:

I think that it's a logical thing to progress into writing songs about subjects like these; Jaguars and Odo-ro-no and all the rest. Instead of putting 'Oh, my heart is breaking', I put 'Oh, my arms are stinking'. At least it makes a change from the usual draggy old love songs, at least it's a bit more relevant to real lives and problems.

I want to take something really improbable, like Odo-ro-no, and write a story that would go beyond being flip and funny, that would have some poignancy about it. It's not easy because everyone's immediate reaction will be to laugh, but it's possible and it would be something worth doing.[2]

Townshends' remarkable pop operetta *A Quick One While He's Away*, which lasts about four times as long as a conventional pop song, shows how successful the Who have been in translating these ideas into hard musical fact. *A Quick One* relates the surrender to temptation of a woman whose husband

[1] *Intro*, 11 November, 1967.
[2] *Intro*, 28 October, 1967.

is absent on business, and quotes musically from Grand Opera, hymn tunes and Western film music. The wife's confessional on her husband's return contains the delightful lines:

> *I sat on Ivor the engine driver's lap*
> *And later with him had a nap.*

You are forgiven chants the husband in unconvincing monotone, a refrain which the whole group takes up in an effervescent parody of a Rossini choral finale.

But the foremost poet within the pop idiom remains Bob Dylan. It took a number of chance happenings to absolve him from the charges of obscurity, self-indulgence and treachery which were levelled at the time of his change of style. First, the arrogant hostility of the audiences who broke up his 1966 British concerts because he would not conform to the folk-singing image they had built of him. Second, his motor-cycle accident later in 1966 (as inevitable, somehow, as the death of the hero in a Greek tragedy), which removed him from the recording world for eighteen months, and provided an opportunity for a cool reassessment of his work.

The insights provided by the concerts, and by the chance to take a retrospective look at his work unbiased by the snap responses to current productions (a rare opportunity in an idiom that is for ever on heat, if not actually breeding), brought a new aspect of Dylan to the fore. It became clear that many of his lyrics were made to seem 'obscure' by one of pop's master-tricks: the assumption we make when confronted by a specifically pop context that what is neither recognizably mythological nor obviously documentary nor just plain straightforward must be obscure. More subtle sub-divisions may exist in the more serious arts, but not, surely, in pop.

So inured were we against the elliptical personal voice in this idiom that many of us did not see Dylan's songs for what they are: reality-based fables. The weird landscapes, the Spanish tarts, the dwarfs and throw-outs that haunt his lyrics are, more often than was ever imagined, particles from his own experience rather than random surrealist symbols. (Though in *John Wesley Harding*, his most recent album at the time of writing, there is a return to a sort of simplicity of lyric and accompaniment. This is not the Woody Guthrie plain-speaking that energizes his early L.P.s, but a brand of clear-cut, almost Bunyanesque, moral allegory. There are strong religious overtones—the titles of his L.P.s always contain a clue to what is going on—and it may be that his near-fatal crash and the subsequent period of enforced introspection had as profound an effect on him as on our attitude towards his previous work.)

In many ways the best of Dylan's songs can stand as prototypes of what pop lyrics should be. Some of their qualities—for instance, their imagic use of the concrete totems of American life—are the results of Dylan's skill as a writer. But his development, say, of the highly-charged, personalized catch-phrase (and his knowledge, obvious enough one would have thought, that lyrics seem more personal the closer the singer is to the microphone) is something from which all pop songwriters, regardless of talent, could learn. In the blues this was always a channel through which an illiterate but sincere voice could find expression; the solution may be an apt one for our writers, too.

Two final points about this book. I have, wherever possible, tried to choose articles which elaborate on the changes which I have hinted at in this Introduction. What I have not considered in any great detail is the organization side of the business. I would justify this omission on the grounds that behind-the-scenes manipulation and financial wizardry have very little relevance to the overall shape of the scene. The audience does choose, and the choices which it makes are clearly influenced by the meaning which pop music holds for them. It is this meaning that the book attempts to explore.

Postscript*

As I write, there is a new excitement in the air. With a flattering regard for the symmetry of this book the cycle of fashion has come full circle and resurrected old-style rock'n'roll. Bill Haley and the Comets are booked for a British tour; Radio One is

* Spring, 1968.

reviving stacks of old Eddie Cochrane, Buddy Holly and Little Richard singles; the Beatles, still cannily commercial in spite of their growing concentration on spiritual matters, have issued a rock single, *Lady Madonna*. Even skiffle groups and buskers are being given a second hearing. There's no doubt, I think, that this can be read as a welcome reaction against the flabbiness of flower music. There's equally no doubt that within a very short space of time something else will have replaced it in the limelight.

2 Survey*

A fairy tale for our time

Cinderella—now Kathy, aged seventeen—works in a boutique
in Whitechapel. Her own clothes, which she designs and makes
herself, are indistinguishable from the ones she sells. In the
evenings she goes to a rhythm-and-blues club in the West End.
Prince Charming—now Mick, aged eighteen and untitled—
plays the organ in the resident group. He was once an apprentice in a large electrical firm, until his group won a talent contest
sponsored by a TV show. He now earns more than his former
managing director. Mick notices Kathy dancing with three
other girls and in the interval comes down from the stand to
dance with her. At midnight they have to rush away, not home,
but to a club in St James, where Mick's group has another
engagement. Kathy and Mick walk down that exclusive street
with a confidence that would embarrass their parents.

An agent who looks in likes the sound of Mick's group and
signs them up for an American tour. As a celebration present
Mick sets Kathy up in her own boutique just off Regent Street.
The clothes she designs soon become so popular that she too is
invited to America. She celebrates her eighteenth birthday with
Mick at the New York Hilton.

There may or may not be a Kathy and Mick who fit this story
exactly. But there could be, and nobody would be surprised.

* January, 1966.

And in contrast to the original story—and, for that matter, to the British scene of only ten years ago—Kathy would need no miraculous help in her rise to the Rooftop Bar.

A great deal has happened in those ten years. The pop music scene has become an arena in which the old lodestar divisions of class, age, sex, status and geography have been challenged and uprooted. The marks of this economic, social and cultural upheaval are everywhere around us. (And around everybody else: a hit record in this country will almost certainly end up being a hit in a dozen other countries from Norway to Nigeria.) No music before has ever been so limited in style yet so ubiquitous in influence. Three-year-olds whistle complex pop tunes in the streets; factories relay them to increase production, and supermarkets to increase consumption. Pubs, clothes shops and even launderettes now have their own juke boxes. Six pirate radio stations playing nothing but pop sprang up round the English coast to satisfy the demands of an estimated 20 million listeners. So pervasive has the sound of pop become that one serious composer I know despairs of ever being able to escape its influence in his work.

Socially, its power is enormous. Ever since rock'n'roll arrived in this country in 1956, pop music has been the main cultural diet of most British teenagers. It has shaped their ambitions, their values, their language and their clothes. In the pop singer, for instance, the young have found a new type of hero and the old a new type of scapegoat. Some singers, like Mick Jagger, have experienced the full implications of this, and have been the centres of the sort of disturbance usually reserved for saints and dictators.

Around these idols, preying on their popularity and image, has grown a fantastic parasite industry. Today you can have your favourite singer's face on your wallpaper, T-shirt, stockings, popcorn packet and writing paper. You could have entered a competition in which the prize was tea with the Dave Clark Five, bought a piece of the floor on which the Beatles used to play in Liverpool's Cavern Club, or used Sonny and Cher cosmetics 'to duplicate her dark-eyed beauty'.

It was the Beatles, of course, who were responsible for

B

starting the Great Pop Boom that kept the voltage at every point
on the pop grid at such a dizzy height between 1963 and 1965.
During this period forty new pop records were being released
every week, and the 6s. 8d. singles were selling over 70 million
copies a year.[1] The Beatles themselves had sold over 115
million records round the world by the autumn of 1965. It
must have been comforting for them to see that, through all
the ballyhoo, people still remembered they were singers. They
had, only three years after playing for their meals in beat clubs
in Hamburg, been called 'our best export' by the Prime
Minister, had a reception given in their honour by Sir David
Ormsby Gore, the British Ambassador in Washington, and
had their wax images placed in Madame Tussauds. Ringo was
elected President of Leeds University in preference to the Lord
Chief Justice, and Western Theatre Ballet danced a piece
called *Mods and Rockers* to a collection of Lennon and
McCartney songs. In June, 1965, the leaders of an Indonesian
dance band were imprisoned for playing 'subversive' Beatles
music. Finally, six months after the legendary M.B.E. awards,
when it was being suggested that the bulk of the Beatles'
audience were now respectable over-twenties, teenage riots
began again at their traditional Christmas show in Finsbury
Park. During the first two nights the number of fainting cases
totalled over 200. The tide of this particular fashion—which
admittedly had never entirely receded—had reached high-
water again after only two years.

When music was popular, not pop

It's with something of a jolt that one remembers we are talking
about *music*. It seems a long way from Finsbury Park to the
certainties of the Palm Court. Pop is not the first popular music
to have spread its influence beyond the dance-hall and the
gramophone. But it is the first to have done so on such a scale,
and with such an indifference to class and sectional barriers.

[1] Though one should not be too overawed by these figures. As early
as 1926, Victoria Spivey's *Black Snake Blues* sold over 150,000 copies
in thirty days.

The Charleston was the centre of a craze which embraced dress fads and wild drinking parties, but its permeation of the working classes never approached that of even the most transient of modern crazes. And the bebop devotees in Harlem in the 'forties had a whole life-style of their own: narcotics, goatee beards, berets, dark glasses and a private hip slang. But they never numbered more than a few hundred.

Pop today has become the focus of a complex teenage sub-culture. The music is no longer something simply to be listened to: it has to be *experienced*. For a start there are the dances. The Jerk, Frug, Bird and Dog, to mention just a few, have bewildered the adult world by their intricacy, lack of grace and apparent asexuality. Some, like the Twist, have become crazes in their own right, and have momentarily taken over the spotlight from the singers and the songs. With the Twist as a dance came Columbia Picture's *Twist Around the Clock* and booklets like *Dance the Twist*. There were twist skirts, twist necklaces and twist dresses. The *Sunday Times* of 4 March, 1962, reported that Mecca Dance halls had been clocking up 10 per cent higher attendances since the craze began, and that a firm in Derby which had produced the first twist shoe had sold 15,000 pairs in two weeks. Clothes, in fact, have always been the most important subsidiary to records in the pop scene. (In fact, money spent on teenage clothes far outstrips that spent on records.) A whole new industry has sprung up to make and sell the uniforms that pop stars and their audiences copy from each other. The boys have their shops in Carnaby Street, and the girls their boutiques in Kensington. The jaunty floral patterns and dayglo P.V.C. that have come out of these modern cottage industries have put Britain back in the forefront of world fashion.

At this point, it becomes necessary to ask a few searching questions about the whole carnival. First, the most basic, what is it about teenage society today that has brought about the creation of this pop scene, that Colin MacInnes has called the 'underground of joy'? Second, is it or was it a spontaneous creation at all? Or has it been skilfully manufactured for teen-agers by an adult world that wants as much as possible of its off-spring's £1,000-million-a-year spending money?

The industry's conspicuous failure ever to *create* a craze successfully tends to make one sceptical about such a concept. Calypso and Cha-Cha, both artificially introduced into this county in the late 'fifties, never achieved anything like the popularity of Skiffle and Merseybeat, which started right on the cellar floor. These were already crazes before they were even noticed by the industry. But whether their subsequent eclipse was a result of the natural swing of fashion, or the unnatural pressures of publicity and commercialization, is a question which recurs with the passing of every new trend.[1]

Which brings us to the final problem. Pop music has considerable *social* demands made upon it. It is this which distinguishes it most clearly from classical music, and even from contemporary jazz. From somewhere in pop's cornucopia must be found dance music to satisfy the athletic demands of millions of well-fed, uninhibited teenagers. There must also be tunes for whistling in the street; so songs must be short, and words and melodies easy to remember. The singers, too, will be judged on more than their pure musical ability. Their choice of songs, their hair, faces, clothes, movements, gestures and private lives, will all be taken into account.

Yet need this affect the quality of the music in the way it so often seems to? Is there any good reason why music which is functional should not also be musical, any real excuse for the danceable sounds of an attractive young group not being also subtly interesting to listen to? After all, the vigorous Allemands and Galliards of the Elizabethan era were.

The lyrics of the modern pop song are perhaps the saddest comment of all:

> *Tonight's the night I've waited for,*
> *Because you're not a baby any more.*

[1] Though a limited amount of commercialisation is inevitable and probably harmless. Even serious music has had to endure this since the advent of the L.P. The 'Top Twenty Classics'—'Everyone a must' —is now advertised in most record shops. Vying for the top in my local at the moment are Tchaikovsky's 1812, and the Red Army Choir. If this makes more people buy the 1812, so much the better. Certainly Tchaikovsky is not diminished musically by being dragged into a Hit Parade, and by being beaten by the Red Army at that.

You've grown into the prettiest girl I've ever seen,
Happy birthday sweet sixteen.[1]

It is a curious fact that a generation that has rebelled in almost every way—from shooting policemen for kicks, to going to prison for peace—still has as the main topic of even its most raucous songs this most respectable of subjects. Even the *way* love is sung about is prim, impersonal and uncomplicated. Girls are never actually married in a pop song—only dreaming of it. Nor do they grow old and difficult to live with. Nobody even goes to bed, to use that gentle euphemism which is nevertheless too crude for the pop world. When Elvis Presley sneakily broke the rule, and breathed *One Night With You* into a million living-rooms, most people were so anaesthetized by the genteel conventions of pop that they didn't realize what he was saying.

Nobody would want pop songs to become wholly serious, or even wholly realistic. But at the moment there are virtually no songs that are even imaginatively unrealistic, that could parallel, for instance, the slick inventiveness of *The Avengers*. We have even lost the topical comment song, which was one of the mainstays of popular music right up until the 1930s.

Put me upon an island where the girls are few,
Put me among the most ferocious lions in the zoo;
You can put me on a treadmill and I'll never, never fret,
But for pity's sake, don't put me near a suffragette.

The topical lyric would suit today's songs, existing as they do for not much longer than the memory of a headline. How much brighter and more exciting might the pop music of the 'sixties have been if its tight conventions had allowed through some songs about Christine Keeler, the Clacton battles, the General Election Campaigns and the Great Train Robbery.

It would be easy to demand no more of pop than that it satisfied our legitimate desire for momentarily exciting, disposable experiences, and for the surprises that replace them. Easy, too, not to exceed the less legitimate desire for a stereophonic refuge in which everybody is in love, and the greatest

[1] *Happy Birthday Sweet Sixteen,* Neil Sedaka.

ill that can happen to a man is to have a crush on the Girl of his Best Friend. But every other popular medium has done more than this. Films and television have provoked us, made us ask questions, and been the more entertaining because of it. Song has been alone amongst the popular arts in playing it safe, in having nothing more than electronic echo-chambers and fuzz-boxes to suggest that it belongs to the twentieth century. Perhaps some song about Christine Keeler did materialize in a few Rugby Club changing-rooms. But it certainly never reached the dance-halls, where it would no doubt have been a favourite in the 'nineties. The scandals and laments that were sung by our supposedly prudish forebears have their only equivalent in some of the songs that circulate in folk-music clubs. The interest in these is growing, but their appeal is still a minority one. Only once has the brave attempt of their young singers to create a music that commented on contemporary life had repercussions on the larger world of pop. In the summer of 1965—largely because of the aura and publicity surrounding an American phenomenon by the name of Bob Dylan—social consciousness struck the Hit Parade. Manfred Mann and Donovan put some impressive songs about war into the Top Twenty. But within a few weeks the industry had decided, with awful predictability, that 'protest' music was to be the next rave fashion. After this, as more and more singers put on badges that really didn't suit them, and the songs became more ludicrous and hypocritical, the craze collapsed, over-ridden and undernourished.[1]

Which came first, the piper or the rats?

At every level of the pop scene, fashion plays a central role. Its wilder excesses have been the cause of most of the public concern about pop; its temporary security provides a framework within which old styles can be killed off and new ones introduced; it forms the structure which links singers, songs, clothes and dances; above all, it also links the audience and the

[1] The full story of the significant miscarriage of this most hopeful trend is told in Chapter 5.

industry. It is with these last two junctions that this book is principally concerned. Most trends and crazes in the pop world are partly spontaneous and partly commercially stimulated. But what is the relative importance of these two shaping forces? How is a new craze thrown up amongst teenagers, and in what ways does the industry mould and encourage and perhaps finally destroy it? How much does this manipulation condition teenage tastes? Has it, for instance, encouraged the desire for comfortable lyrics that was mentioned earlier? Centrally, does the word 'popular', when applied to contemporary music, mean 'of the people', or 'thrust down most of their throats'?

This book is an attempt to examine the nature and status of fashion in the pop world today; to look at the sources of trends in teenage society and the pop industry, and at the social and commercial forces that affect their growth. It is also, inevitably, one side of the story of the post-war professional teenager, that much-discussed young person who demands to be seen *and* heard, who spends half her wages on clothes, runs her own TV shows, behaves like an old trouper after only six months in the business, yet can still bring herself to scream as lustily as her twelve-year-old sister. If on the brighter side the story is one of gaiety, colour and community, on the darker it is one of immaturity, narrow-mindedness and conformity. Rock'n'roll and its subsequent variations developed against a background of worldwide teenage unrest, and the scene built on them shares all the equivocal shades of meaning of that upheaval.

3   The roots*

Dear Beatles,
    Wilton, Connecticut, is a small town. Nothing ever happens here. Oh, once Raymond Massey lived here, but he moved away because he couldn't stand it.
    If only you could drive through Wilton, it would never be the same again.
    We need help! Everybody is falling asleep here.
                   Love, Jennifer C.[1]

The most popular record in Britain during the autumn of 1955 was Slim Whitman's *Rose Marie*. When Ken Dodd's *Tears* rose to the same position exactly ten years later, it might have seemed that, for all the uproar, nothing had really changed in pop music. But Ken Dodd was an exception; Slim Whitman the rule. The Hit Parade during the latter months of 1955 consisted almost entirely of cheery fireside songs like *Twenty Tiny Fingers*, *Oh Mein Papa* and *The Happy Wanderer*, performed by artists like the Stargazers, Eddie Calvert and Dickie Valentine.

    We still have these songs and these artists, just as we still have, caught in a tea-break and Sunday afternoon limbo, brass bands, pub songs, buskers, Winifred Atwell, Nellie Dean, the Luton Girls' Choir, the foxtrot, Rodgers and Hammerstein, the Salvation Army and Tony Evan's Tea Dance in the Leicester Square Mecca. Popular music these may be; pop music, to use that increasingly confusing abbreviation, they manifestly

* December, 1965.
[1] *Love Letters to the Beatles*, Anthony Blond, 1964.

are not. But only a functional definition can separate them with any precision. All popular music is concerned with participation, with parties, dances, outings, demonstrations and any other social gatherings where camaraderie and simple shared emotions are important. The impact of most popular music increases with the size and degree of cohesion of the audience, and this is not just because of the mildly hysterical atmosphere which can be generated inside any large gathering. The music, in fact, acts as a further binding-force on the group, and the observed responses of the other members are a way of clarifying your own. (We have here, incidentally, another differentiation from 'classical' music, which is fundamentally a tradition of individual and personal experiences. It makes little difference when you are playing or listening to Bach whether the audience is one or a thousand.)

Pop music, as a sub-division of popular, is that which operates as one of the common languages of the 'scene'. The latter is a network of institutions, operating almost exclusively to satisfy teenage tastes, which is characterized, as we will see later, by the intricate relationships between its parts. Boutiques and beat clubs are owned by the same people, singers crib new fashions from dancers, and film companies build whole movies around eighteen-year-olds. The qualification for entry to the scene is consequently the adoption of the currently fashionable norm in just *one* of the basic variables: music, idols, clothes or dance.

There was no pop 'scene' in the early 'fifties, and the music, however quaint it may seem now, was listened to by teenager and magistrate alike. There are no accounts of young people copying Ambrose's hairstyle or Max Bygrave's clothes, and there were certainly very few popular singers who were under the age of thirty. Unlike their parents during the extravagant years of the Jazz Age, the austere young things of the 'fifties did not feel that music, dancing, clothes and social behaviour had very much to do with each other.

There were a few exceptions. Ever since a momentous concert at the Carnegie Hall in 1943, a large number of young girls had found that one gaunt American singer had the power to make them very excited indeed. His name was Frank Sinatra. They begged for his old ties, tore off his specially-weakened suits, and cut pieces out of the carpets he walked on. Whenever he sang at the Paramount Theatre the ushers used to carry smelling salts to revive the swooning girls. But the majority of even the most voracious of Sinatra's fans were much older than the average pop fan today. (This was also true of the fans who mobbed Frankie Laine and Johnnie Ray. In *Fan Fever*, a film made by Associated-Rediffusion in 1958, the members of the Johnnie Ray Fan Club—'Appreciation Society', they insisted on calling it—appeared predominantly to be young women between the ages of twenty and twenty-five.) By contemporary pop music standards Sinatra's early songs were sophisticated and musical. They had elaborate orchestral backings and an aura of transatlantic jet-flights and tenement cocktail-parties. This, for all the fan clubs and the mobbing, was hardly the sort of music to turn on the working-class youth of Britain.

Omens from the East

If popular music provided no social focus for the young people of the early 'fifties, the society of the street did little better. What social life there was, was geographical, based on the local chip-shops and cafés. There was no concept of 'teenagers' as a class apart, and little importance was attached to fashion, whether in dance, dress or social behaviour. Moreover, 'respectable' teenage girls were almost entirely absent from the clannish street life of the young men.

The happiest consequence of this lack of social cohesion amongst the young was the absence of that deliberate, anxious group conformity that is so marked today. What might have seemed like conformity was, in fact, unavoidable uniformity, a result of the relative poverty of young people and the small range of leisure-time activities open to them. There were still boys wearing cloth-caps in the early 'fifties, and they were spending many of their evenings, like their fathers, on street corners. In most areas the only alternatives to this were a puritanical youth-club or an expensive pub. Consequently it was not surprising that these bored young men occasionally, for the fags, the money and the sheer thrill, prized a cigarette machine off some tradesman's wall.

The New Towns and modern housing estates, for all their promise, seemed only to aggravate the lack of community amongst the young. The American-inspired milk-bars and coffee-bars that were springing up with them made for a partial remedy, with the relief that their drinks and nickelodeons provided from the monotony of street life. They were cheap, warm and moderately friendly. But they added no new elements to teenage life; as social centres or places for entertainment they tended to be lifeless and hollow.

Portents of the radical changes in teenage life that were imminent came from two directions. The first from London's East End, in the shape of that now legendary figure, the Teddy Boy. The expression was, strictly speaking, a sartorial one, used to describe those young men of the time who dressed in long drape jackets with velvet collars, elaborately decorated waistcoats, skin-tight trousers, and shoes with two-inch thick crepe soles. But it soon came to be a term of abuse to be thrown at any conspicuously dressed youth who looked as if he might be a potential hooligan.

The Teddy Boy craze seems, by all reports, to have started in the Elephant and Castle in about 1954. This in itself was unusual, for the East Enders had a tradition of spirited resistance to social change. They had certainly never bothered much about clothes before, least of all about the rather effeminate (some thought) frippery of velvet collars and silk waistcoats. (With its inspiration deriving from Edwardian England the fashion was, moreover, a complete reversal of the then current trend towards gentle Americanization.)

The male debs of Kensington and Knightsbridge had been the first to wear Edwardian clothes. The East End boys, on their weekend sorties over the river, cannot have failed to notice them, and in an act of rebellion which, however unconsciously, attacked with one sweep of a drape-coat-tail the 'nobs's' prerogative of elegance, the austerity of the post-war urban environment, and the old working-class virtue of 'knowing your place', they started to copy the rudiments of the fashion. The version they evolved was less tasteful but more economic, and in less than a year they were manipulating styles as confidently as any Savile Row habitué. Hugh Latymer, writing in the *Observer* in 1955, described one Ted he had met who had built up his suit from the pages of *Man About Town*, taking the coat from one page and the waistcoat from another.

Whatever the needs which aroused the Elephant and Castle boys, they had clearly been lurking not far under the surface of many young people. For the fashion spread phenomenally as soon as it was publicized. Most of the publicity came not so much from the eccentricity of the dress as from the acts of violence and hooliganism committed by a few of its wearers. A great deal of the criticism of this behaviour was undoubtedly fair; the temperament which could enable barely adult men to break away from a centuries'-old tradition of dress could hardly be a reserved one. Moreover, the unusualness of the dress attracted a great deal of staring and ridicule, which was countered in the age-old way. But there is equally no doubt that, because the Teds were a highly distinctive minority group, their violence was noticed much more than that of the less ostentatious. They represented more in those confused times than a simple, though unusually colourful, variation on the delinquent theme.

Omens from the West

1956 was a full year: the Hungarian people rose against their government, the British blundered into Suez and, in a kind of response in advance, *Look Back in Anger* happened at the Royal Court Theatre. It was also the year in which a rather mediocre film called *Rock Around the Clock* arrived in this country from America. *Rock Around the Clock* was a musical featuring a band called Bill Haley and the Comets. The plot was simple: a group of country musicians (The Comets) decide that dance music has become too sluggish, and 'invent' a new dance music called rock'n'roll, which is loud and fast, and in which the whole burden of the rhythm leans on the off-beat.

Rock is discovered by an itinerant agent, is plugged incessantly and becomes a coast-to-coast craze.

In spite of the fact that Britain had had an unspectacular foretaste of this music (the title number had appeared in a film called *Blackboard Jungle* in 1954, and had been top of the Hit Parade at the beginning of 1956), *Rock Around the Clock* arrived surrounded by rumour and expectancy. There had been large-scale disturbances in the United States at cinemas where the film was being shown. One commentator had summed up the opinions of most adults when he wrote: 'It does for music what a motor-cycle club at full throttle does for a Sunday afternoon.'

The music wasn't new, though. The relentless back beat, the chunky, amplified guitar sound and the responsorial saxophone phrases punctuating the singer's lines were all characteristic of the urban blues style that had been developing in the Memphis area since the late 'forties and early 'fifties. The punchy music played by Joe Turner, Floyd Dixon, T-Bone Walker and Percy Mayfield was in all respects the guts of rock'n'roll. To produce the final product, singers like Elvis Presley, many of whom had come from a white rural background of gospel meetings and barn dances, wedded this sound to their own more gentle country styles. But it would be a hard task to trace the exact route which this musical amalgam travelled down through the Mississippi Basin to gain, eventually, world-wide publicity from Hollywood, California.

Rock Around the Clock opened in Britain at the beginning of September, 1956. How it was received in one cinema in the North was described in *New Society* by an ex-member of a Liverpool street gang:

> The queue outside the Palais was large but quite orderly. There were many gangs present, but the pact of neutral territory held good.
>
> Gangs filed in and filled up row after row. Unlike most of the films, this one had commanded an almost entirely adolescent audience. When the music started it was infectious—no-one managed to keep still. It was the first time the gangs had been exposed to an animal rhythm that matched their behaviour. Soon

couples were in the aisles copying the jiving on the screen. The 'bouncers' ran down to stop them. The audience went mad. Chairs were pulled backwards and forwards, arm rests uprooted, in an unprecedented orgy of vandalism. There were fourteen seats missing when it was 'Queenie' time.[1]

By the middle of September there had been sixty arrests following riots at showings, and thirteen major towns and cities had banned the film from their cinemas on the grounds that it was 'likely to cause a public disturbance'. On the Continent the riots were frequently spectacular. In Copenhagen, gangs of boys were singing and dancing in the streets for four days after a performance. In one German riot (which occurred after a cinema had cancelled a performance), teenagers closed the main street at both ends and held motor-cycle races in it. Back in Cheshunt, England, Harry Webb (later to become Cliff Richard) lost his prefect's badge for playing truant to see Bill Haley.

The pattern of the disturbances was temporal, not geographical, and a great deal of the trouble was obviously due to inflated publicity. At least 300 towns had shown the film before there were any riots at all. The publicity also introduced an element of competition between teenage groups in different districts. But there were more significant motives behind the riots than a mere desire for notoriety. As one youth said in a London Courtroom after a cinema disturbance: 'If only they would show *Rock Around the Clock* in dance-halls, without seats, then we could really enjoy it.' Ultimately, rock'n'roll, like the blues from which it was derived, was an antidote to to frustration as well as an expression of it.

The arrival of sound

But cinema-seats were the least important things to be disturbed by rock'n'roll.

[1] Colin Fletcher 'Beat and Gangs on Merseyside', 20 February, 1964. To my knowledge this is the only serious first-hand account of the effect on British teenagers of the arrival of rock'n'roll. Consequently, I shall be quoting from it on a number of other occasions.

. . . the beat spread like a rumour; the interpretations were more important than the original. Saturday night had always been the climax of the week when boots were exchanged for polished shoes and a truce was called to allow free movement across town and city. The Saturday night meeting time had always been 7 o'clock but it was suddenly changed to 7.30 p.m. This radical move was caused by B.B.C.'s new contribution to the passing craze *6-5 Special*.

This show was very important, because it was more amateurish, as were all British attempts at the time, and this made copying very much easier. There were more 'numbers' to choose from and the guitar started wholly to replace trumpets and saxophones. Elvis Presley's *Heartbreak Hotel* realized the potential of a barrage of guitars. Slightly later Buddy Holly and the Crickets made the point eminently clear with their first record, *That'll be the Day*. Ten members of the Park Gang bought this record—starting a habit that they were unlikely to give up—and the musical element found the hammering thrown-out beat easy and most enjoyable to imitate. Guitars and a set of drums were needed to succeed in a reasonable rendering but this idea was only a suggestion for four months.[1]

These effects were felt over the whole country, and the changes which they brought about in popular music seem to have been permanent. Teenagers looked at the groups lustily playing their guitars, and saw something which was not only easier to imitate, but which was more exciting to watch than an orchestra seated at their music stands. So amateurism (*not amateurishness and bum notes*) started to replace the silky professionalism of Ray Conniff and Bing Crosby. Coupled with this came a growing veneration for the sheer *sound* of a record, for the total aural effect produced by the ryhthm of the words, the tone of the instruments and the ingenuity of the recording engineer.

The sound which was characteristic of rock'n'roll at this stage, and which has become the foundation of most pop music since, was produced by a number of amplified instruments playing basically as percussion. A typical group might consist of two electric guitars, string bass, drums, piano and

[1] Colin Fletcher, *op. cit.*

saxophone. The bass and drums would be played with a heavy emphasis on the off-beat; one of the guitars and the piano would add to this by crayoning in rhythmic vamped chords, whilst the other guitar might add melodic embellishments, and improvise a solo between the verses. The saxophone's main function was to provide richness and body to the chordal structure and a voice to shout back at the singer—congregation to preacher. Upon this basic sound most of the early rock singers and groups imposed their own personal modulations. Fats Domino's was honeyed and relaxed, yet as relentless as a well-oiled grandfather clock; Little Richard's was frenzied and throaty; Buddy Holly's, wistful and clean-cut.

As the sound became more important and dancing the key activity which pop music had to sustain, so the lyrics inevitably diminished in importance. They soon became little more than pegs on which to hang the music, exhortations whose function was to underline the compulsiveness of the music. Some were jingles based on a key idea or catch-phrase title, like Presley's *All Shook Up*, and Bill Haley's *See You Later, Alligator*.

> *See you later alligator,*
> *In a while crocodile,*
> *Don't you know you're in my way now,*
> *Can't you see you cramp my style.*

The more narrative songs, like Marty Wilde's *Teenager in Love*,[1] Craig Douglas's *Only Sixteen* and Tab Hunter's *Young Love* were usually formula representations of some presumed aspect of the teenage condition: 'If you go away I'll cry'; 'If you don't go away I'll cry'; 'Mum and Dad don't understand'; 'Why did you dance with that other boy?' In the tens of thousands of songs of this sort that have been written over the past ten years, the same set scenes have been recounted over and over again, each time in just slightly different words. The songwriters seem to have been as anxious to keep their personalities out of their

---

[1] The disregard for the content of pop songs has become so institutionalized that we label songs purely in terms of their performers, who are only in exceptional cases the writers as well.

lyrics as the singers have been to put them into their performances.

Rock'n'roll was the first nation-wide musical craze that had belonged exclusively to the teenager. Commercial pressures did exist, and many professional British musicians turned their dance-bands into rock combos. But the fashion swept itself along faster than the exploiters could follow. Most significant of all was the desire of young people not just to listen, but to take part. Colin Fletcher's gang, like many others all over the country, eventually formed its own group.

In June, 1958, following the trend, the Park Gang gave birth to the Tremeloes. There had been excited anticipation when four of the musical element started to learn to play the guitar. The gang had no real notion of what a rock group looked like until these boys came down to the shed with their instruments one night and played for half an hour. The gang jived on the grass and clapped wildly after every item. . . . Soon it became a regular thing for the gang actively to support every practice. The group was becoming the gang's totem. The gang had started to rival other gangs on a totally new level. As the process of producing a group from within a gang's ranks was cumulative one could feel the decline of tension in other forms of competition. What mattered now was not how many boys a gang could muster for a Friday night fight but how well their group played on Saturday night. . . . The Park Gang literally nursed its group. To enable the group to buy microphones and speakers a system of 'shares' was set up which were to be repaid from the group's earnings. Any member of the gang could buy any number of shares and in this way help the group to compete successfully with the groups of rival gangs. The trusted 'spiritual' boys became the director and manager respectively. An electrical apprentice acted as an on-the-spot repairer when the amplifiers or guitar pick-ups failed. . . . Girls, too, assumed a new role. They became seamstresses. The group needed uniforms and yet could not afford the £100 for a set of four beat outfits. These beginnings of idomatic clothing were within the group, though soon the gang identified itself with the group by copying the group's clothes.[1]

[1] Colin Fletcher, *op. cit.*

'Some folks call it a garbage can, but I call it a streamline bass'   (Will Shade)

But the real participant craze of the late 'fifties was not rock'n' roll but that musical anomaly, skiffle. Skiffle was aptly christened 'The do-it-yourself folk-music'. You played it with any instruments—and indeed objects—that happened to be available, and the songs that were most widely used were the blues, dance-tunes and folk ballads of North America. Skiffle—style, instrumentation and word itself—was a product of the American slump, and its progress to reincarnation in a booming Britain makes an intriguing story.

During the Depression musical instruments became a luxury for most American negroes. With wages in Mississippi down to as little as three dollars a week it was as much as most could do to afford food. But music will out, and particularly a music which, like blues and gospel song, has been important in providing an oppressed minority with a common language of protest and hope. So the Mississippi Negroes raided the junk shops which were stuffed with instruments from the demobilized Confederate military bands, or, failing that, made their own. They blew into jugs, bottles and garbage cans and produced remarkable imitations of the sounds of a brass section. They stretched animal skins across turtle-shells and made banjos. Muddy Waters used an old box.

> All the kids made their own git-tars. Made mine out of a box and a bit of stick for a neck. Couldn't do much with it but you know, that's how you learn . . . but my first real instrument was the harp.[1] Well I played everywhere I could—any ole place. Jukes around Clarks-dale. Played for those Sat'dy night fish-fries. I used to sell fish too, then go to playin'. Everybody used to fry up fish and had one hell of a time. Find me workin' all night, playin', workin' till sunrise for fifty cents and a sandwich and be glad of it, and they really like the low down blues.[2]

The fish-fries were only one way of beginning: using sometimes a guitar and sometimes a cigar-box and a piece of wire,

[1] Negro term for a mouth organ.
[2] Paul Oliver, *Conversations with the Blues*, Cassell, 1964.

the Muddy Waters and Skinny Head Petes would play in barber's shops, excursion trains and medicine shows; to trippers embarking from boats, and mourners going home from funerals.

But it was at a function known as the rent party that these *ad-hoc* collections of musicians and their bizarre instruments appeared most frequently. During the slump, wages were so low that 4 dollars a month rent for an unfurnished three-room shack could be crippling. When there was clearly not going to be enough money to pay, a group of families used to pool their savings and hold a party, charging their neighbours a few cents admission, and providing them with a barrel or two of bootleg gin, or raw wood-alcohol laced with cheap sherry. At these parties anyone who could play—whether it was a harmonica or a washboard—helped out with the music. Nothing was ruled out: negro work-songs, white gospel-songs, French quadrilles and Irish ballads were all thrown in as the Rot-Gut loosened tongues and inhibitions.

Skiffle or spasm—as this music came to be called—was more a style of playing than a musical form in its own right. Nevertheless, it had a distinctive if rather scatty sound and, thanks to some of the early Negro groups like Ma Rainey and the Tub Jug Washboard Band, a few original numbers to its credit. Consequently, during the New Orleans Jazz revival of the early 'fifties and the accompanying wave of interest in traditional negro music,[1] a number of British bands formed skiffle groups from amongst their members. The Crane River Jazz Band formed a group as early as 1949, and was followed by that corner-stone of British jazz, the Ken Colyer Jazzmen. But it was the group that Chris Barber formed in 1954 that was to launch skiffle upon a British public that had never even heard of the word.

Late in 1955 the Chris Barber Skiffle Group released a

[1] Though American negroes were by no means the only depressed people to have made their own music in this way. During the General Strike of 1926, miners from the South Wales coal-fields made kazoos out of metal pipes, borrowed drums from the Boys Brigade, and, wearing fancy clothes made by their wives, paraded round the stricken areas.

recording of a song that had previously been on one of their L.P.s. It was called *Rock Island Line* and was a powerful but lighthearted number about a railway that ran to New Orleans, and the devices that were used by the engine-drivers to avoid the toll payments. It had previously been recorded by Huddie Ledbetter (better known as Leadbelly), an almost mythological Negro singer who had been twice jailed for murder, but dramatically reprieved by the Governor of Louisiana because of his musical talents. On the Barber recording, *Rock Island Line* was sung by Lonnie Donegan, the band's twenty-four-year-old banjoist. The accompaniment was simple: Donegan's own guitar, a washboard and a double bass.

In spite of its rather specialist appeal *Rock Island Line* was played on a couple of radio record programmes. The result was startling: the B.B.C. was flooded with requests for the record to be played again, and for details of the singer and the song. By the spring of 1956, *Rock Island Line* had sold a million copies round the world and reached the number four position in the Hit Parade. There was no precedent for this sort of success for a folk-music record. Lonnie Donegan sang with no concession at all to currently popular tastes. His voice was high, nasal and negroid. His group had no amplifiers and no melody instruments. Yet their pulsing guitar sound cannot have failed to remind listeners of another record with a similar name that had been top of the charts only a few weeks before.

But if the success of *Rock Island Line* was unusual, the craze that sprang from it was unique. The popular press found the song and the way it was performed interesting enough to be worth investigating more thoroughly. They soon discovered that skiffle had something of a pedigree, and a glamorous one at that. But the stories they printed of rent parties and basses made out of beer barrels only served to consolidate a trend that was already under way. After a decade of Vera Lynn, Lonnie Donegan's personal dynamism and the fun, excitement and obvious simplicity of his music were too much to resist. Guitar and banjo sales soared. The country's grocers were besieged by young men demanding washboards, barrels, tea-chests and broom handles. Thousands of skiffle groups were literally nailed together, as if they were Arks to escape the treacle floods that had been pouring out of the radio for just too long. The B.B.C. started a Saturday morning programme called *Skiffle Club* to provide music for the fans, and a forum for the growing number of semi-professional groups like Les Hobeaux and the Vipers. Dr Vivian Fuchs was greeted by a hastily assembled skiffle group when he arrived at the South Pole. Adventurous priests held skiffle Masses in their churches. And in Skegness, one Barry Barron won the Butlin's Camp Skiffle Contest with a group whose instruments were a tea-chest, a dustbin lid, a tin wastepaper basket and an oxtail-soup tin filled with stones.

My own initiation into pop music was via a skiffle group and I can remember vividly the lengths to which we would go for an opportunity to play, the frantic bicycle rides down after cricket to nab the school hall, the pleading interviews with parents for the loan of a Sunday afternoon practice room. We had no ambitions beyond achieving the admiration of our immediate friends, and no desire to play anywhere more grand than the village hall. But, for all that, we had the same compulsive need to perform in public as we had to play solely for our own enjoyment, and there was little to which we would not stoop to achieve this. I can recall paying softening-up donations to the social secretaries of organizations we despised, squeezing into unaccustomed dinner jackets, even hiding a rival group's instruments at a summer evening fête.

I mention these reminiscences, not because of any overpowering nostalgia, but because I think they underline one of the reasons for skiffle's demise. The flavour of a Greyfriars romp, of a long-drawn-out summer picnic, permeated the whole of the skiffle era. Our group certainly had no deep theories about what we were playing, or about the nature of folk music. We were simply concerned to enjoy ourselves. True, we had picked up a few catch-phrases about 'authenticity' and, as if to testify to the purity of our music, we would don, at public performances, the tartan shirts and jeans of the Tennessee country hick. In retrospect it is clear that we were doing no more than imitating the clothes of the groups we had seen on television. For precisely the same reason, our songs were almost all early American: railroad songs, cowboy ballads, Appalachian fiddle-tunes and rural blues. These were the accepted currency of skiffle. Not one group, to my knowledge, ever wrote or sang a song about contemporary Britain.

Understandably this party atmosphere, lacking the sustenance of any new ideas, soon began to pall. Lonnie Donegan had three successive Number Ones, including the memorable *Putting on the Style*, but then abruptly dropped the word skiffle from the title of his group. Slowly the combos began to break up. Some of the renegade members became solo folk-singers, feeling there was more intellectual and artistic satisfaction to be found amongst the grass-roots music on which skiffle was based. Many more, like Jet Harris and Hank Marvin of the Vipers, formed rock'n'roll groups.[1] The commercialists tried to avert the collapse with manœuvres intended to spread skiffle to a wider audience. But in fact they only served to accelerate it: raucous work songs simply sounded ridiculous against a lush orchestral backing.

The key reason for the decline of skiffle was given inadvertently by a man who had prophesied it would never happen. The Rev. Brian Bird had written a book about the craze, and in it predicted: 'Skiffle will continue . . . our skifflers are drawing their material from the right sources—the folk-music of the great Afro-American and British tradition, a rich storehouse of people's music which is almost inexhaustible. They are singing and playing from the heart, and not out of books.'[2] Unfortunately, all the songs that the British skifflers sang *were* out of books, not out of their own experience. Skiffle was fun to play, it was spontaneous, and many of its most popular songs were eloquent to a degree to which rock'n'roll numbers have never been. But the connection between a British teenager of 1959 and a Negro spike-driver of 1929 was a tenuous one. When skiffling teenagers found they could have just as much fun, and twice the nerve-jarring excitement, playing

[1] The Drifters, later to become better known as the Shadows.
[2] *Skiffle*, Brian Bird, Robert Hale, 1958.

through a 60-watt amplifier in a rock group, even the richness of the skiffle songs themselves could not sustain this connection.

Eccentric clothes, guitars, teenage riots, crazes rippling across the country as fast as an anticyclone; the pattern had begun. Inside the social wasteland of the 'fifties, British teenagers had begun to create the scaffolding of an alternative society. It was a temporary and part-time alternative to be sure, existing mostly after dark, and petering out with marriage. But it had its moments of gaiety and community. Rock'n'roll became the barricade of this minor revolution. Not only was it exciting, cathartic and loud, but it was sympathetic to the teenagers' case. It could amuse them, involve them and at the same time express what they were feeling. It became a language, a focal idea to declare allegiance with. And, conveniently, it was also disapproved of by adults.

The nascent pop scene became at this time a bridge between the social life and popular music of young people. Since then, every major fashion in music has been accompanied by an entourage of heroes, clothes and dances, and sometimes even whole new *personae*, like those of the Beatnik and the Mod. The laws and customs of the local gang are no longer supremely influential. Since 1956 they have been steadily replaced by the less personal but geographically unbounded pressures of fashion.

But our central question remains. The initial reactions to skiffle and rock'n'roll were an understandable response to the intolerable boredom of *Workers' Playtime* and the Palais. But how much was the spread of these fashions—and of the economically plumper, socially more obsessive fads that began with the Beatles—a result of commercial manipulation, and how much a result of the desire to conform on a large scale that seemed to be an integral part of this new pattern? In their genuine desire to participate, teenagers not only revived some of the brighter undersurfaces of our rusty popular culture, but became highly vulnerable to conformist pressures, from whichever direction they came.

The next two chapters will consider some of the ways in which fashions—following the pattern set by these prototypes in the 'fifties—are propagated and spread in the pop scene today.

Part Two

4   Sources of fashion: the audience*

In 1959 two American pop promoters, Joe Mulhall and Paul Neff, sent out a questionnaire to 3,000 young people in an attempt to discover their image of a perfect teenage idol. They described the composite picture that emerged in the February, 1960, issue of *Photoplay*:

> A boy who sings well ... not too polished but well. About 5 ft 7 ins tall, of Italian descent (because they look so romantic). Fine build and nice smile; sharp sports clothes; intelligent, considerate of others, sincere, honest and quiet.

After the poll they started searching for a boy to fit the image. Eventually they discovered fifteen-year-old Johnny Restivo from a photograph in a physical culture magazine. To their delight they found he also sang. Johnny Restivo was subsequently groomed and sent out to work, and in a short while became a pop star of the second rank.

The computer-like manufacture of sincere, sharp, romantic Johnny is a microcosm of the way in which many sceptics imagine the pop scene as a whole operates. They see an enormous and absurdly prosperous army of gullible youngsters, whose simple whims can be measured and manipulated by any astute shark, young or old. But the redeeming feature of Mulhall and Neff's dubious social experiment was that Restivo never *really* made it. His career was neither particularly successful nor very long. Which suggest that really popular stars are either more genuinely 'of the people' than this, or that they have an

* January, 1966.

heroic influence over their followers that is not definable by market research.

The hot-houses of fashion

Another over-simplification which has been common amongst pop commentators—particularly those on the quality Sundays —has been the tendency to regard fashions on the pop scene as being universal. Papers normally as acute as the *Financial Times* have fallen into generalizations as sweeping as this one of December 1965:

> Teenage tastes are in another state of revolution. For confirma-
> tion, you need only listen to the latest Beatles' L.P.—it's bound
> to be forced on you sometime this Christmas anyway. The two
> tracks of greatest significance are *Michelle* and *Girl*, both of
> which have much in common with what is happening in the Hit
> Parade at the moment. In place of the heavy brow beat, they are
> simple and sweet.[1]

What was happening in the Hit Parade then was—as always—more complex than this. The Beatles have included 'simple and sweet' numbers on *all* their L.P.s (e.g. *Anna, Yesterday, Till There was You*). And an analysis of the Top Twenty of the week after this comment was published, would hardly have suggested that ballads were at last effecting their counter-revolution: there were thirteen assorted beat numbers, two comedy songs, one orchestral piece, and four ballads. You would find the same proportions in almost any Hit Parade since 1957.

Often there is evidence in the Top Twenty of as many as half-a-dozen different trends at work, some new, some well established. The post-1956 pop scene has its characteristic homogeneity because all its fashions follow a similar pattern, not because there is always one key trend which is slavishly adhered to by every teenager from Liverpool to Clacton. The craze which is newest, which is receiving all the publicity and plugs, is not necessarily the most popular. (And it will certainly

[1] *Financial Times*, 24 December, 1965

not be the one which self-styled teenage élites in London clubs regard as being the most fashionable.) Even rock'n'roll, in spite of its explosive arrival in this country, took some time to become established in the charts. And there were never more than a couple of skiffle records in the Top Twenty at any time during that fashion's comparatively long life.

It is often forgotten, too, that there is no law which prohibits adults (and indeed those young people between the ages of thirteen and twenty who do not think of themselves as 'teenagers') from buying records. Their favourites are frequently in the charts, producing odd situations like that in October, 1965, when Ken Dodd and the Rolling Stones were at the top of the Hit Parade in consecutive weeks. During the past few years the Top Twenty has included one almost serious version of *Ave Maria*, the anthem written for the 1964 Olympic Games, a Cossak folk-song and a weepy religious number entitled *Deck of Cards*, by Wink Martindale. This was not even a song, but a narrative to music about an American soldier who remembered the teachings of the Good Book by means of a deck of cards. ('Five for the Foolish Virgins', etc.)

But the exposure areas—the record sales charts, the TV and radio shows—are not by themselves a comprehensive index of current trends. Between the years 1959 and 1962, when the most conspicuous type of song was the ballad, the music that was being played in the clubs and dance-halls was almost solid rock'n'roll. In the summer of 1965, to take another period at random, the most significant trend in the Hig Parade was the appearance of a handful of folk and protest songs. Yet at the same time the Beatles were at Number One, the journalists were discussing the possible resurgence of ballads, and in the most fashionable discothèques the mods were still listening to Negro vocal groups from Detroit.

The clubs, discothèques and dance-halls, where the innovators and their followers meet, are fertile breeding-grounds for new fashions. As night-out places, they are especially conducive to prodigious clothes and unorthodox dances. They are crucial, too, in the rise to stardom of new groups. Fans who loyally attend every appearance at a club by their favourites can help push them to the top, as the Marquee Club members did Manfred Mann and the Moody Blues.

There is an immense variety of clubs, and this, coupled with the sense of exclusiveness with which their habitués invest them, means that there can be a number of trends which are simultaneously 'fashionable'. (I know a group of young people from North London who once discovered a wild traditional jazz scene in the depths of the Fens, and for whom trad has ever since been 'just on the way back, boy'. In 1964, according to a survey, there were twenty-eight clubs in London alone, with a listed membership of 100,000 and a total weekly attendance of 10,000. Some were churchy little places like Croydon's Georgian, two upstairs rooms with floral wallpaper and china ornaments, where Young Socialists sell their papers in the interval and elderly Mums serve behind the bar. Others were exclusive night-spots like the Ad Lib and the In-Place, where pop stars and those fans that could afford the cover charge stared at each other until the early morning. There are also perennial curiosities like the Top Rank Dance Suites. In spite of their holiday-camp mixture of luxurious furnishing and detention-centre rules, these regularly tempt in audiences of over a thousand. But you must be wearing a tie, a collar, and a jacket *with* lapels. And there are a team of ex-wrestling bouncers to make sure you don't stand on the dance-floor unless you make the appropriate movements with a partner.

London has traditionally been the starting-point of new trends and crazes. It has shops which sell imported records from the States, art schools that run special courses on fashion, and a large teenage population to take advantage of both. Being the First City it also has an authoritative glamour and an anonymity that encourage originality and outrageousness.

But London is by no means unchallenged: trends that have become popular in some provincial club can seep out over a wide area. As well as the Merseyside Wat Tylers who captured London in 1963, Birmingham's Spencer Davis Group, Tyneside's Animals and Dublin's Them all had large local followings before they moved south.

The clubs themselves are difficult to describe; each one's

characteristic flavour changes as rapidly as everything else in pop. But to try to give a small insight into the chameleon habits of the pop audience and into the atmospheres in which new fashions can originate and spread, I have included below short sketches of three clubs: one in London, one in Liverpool and one in a small country town. Their accuracy is no more than that of still photographs taken of the same scenes: they show what was in the light for just that moment of time.

The Cavern, Liverpool: August, 1963

The Cavern, when you have succeeded in finding it amongst the warehouses and second-hand bookshops of Liverpool's commercial quarter, is something of a disappointment. There are no neon signs, no giant posters. Just a shabby door, barely as high as a man, leading to what were once the servants' quarters of a crumbling old mansion. By the entrance a man tells you that there's no admission except with a member. The first that comes along seems quite willing to take you in, though he walks out again as soon as he has signed the book. Down at the desk the attendants are sending chain-smoking twelve-year-olds home for their birth certificates. No one gets past who looks under fifteen and can't prove otherwise.

At the bottom of the steps you hear probably the most deafening sound pop music has ever known. The Cavern is like a railway tunnel inside, and the sound bounces off the bare brick walls that are literally dripping with the humidity. There are three groups playing tonight, the Four Quarters, the Escorts and the Mojos; with the number of Liverpool's beat groups estimated at 300 there are plenty to choose from.

The audience is unclassifiable: there are office girls, grammar-school boys, beatniks in duffel jackets oblivious of the heat, Northern mods in belted jackets and dead straight trousers, a woman of forty bouncing up and down in her chair, and tough kids in T-shirts from the docks. Within thirty miles of London this combination would almost certainly set off a fight. In this corner of punch-happy Liverpool, though, there is nothing but good humour.

It's not easy to see the Escorts at first. They have no group uniform, and their rough-and-tumble elegance is of the same brand as the audience's. Right up close to the slightly raised stage the girls are throwing jelly babies at them and passing up requests scrawled on pieces of paper. The Escorts have the usual line-up of two guitars, electric bass and drums, and the music that they play is that cheerful mixture of rock'n'roll and rhythm and blues that was soon to be known as Merseybeat.[1] In spite of the excitement this sound is beginning to cause throughout the country, up here they have been listening to it for years.

The Escorts' set finishes, and Bob Wooler, compère and champion of the Cavern, gets on the stage to make some announcements. He has the confidence of a man who knows that the home team is just about to win. He reads out the names of some of the non-Liverpudlians visiting the Cavern that night: girls from Aberystwyth, Dartford and Newcastle. Their names ring out as if they were starlets at a première. There is an atmosphere here of overwhelming local pride. Bob Wooler announces that the Escorts are off to London the next day to make their first record. The audience cheers. 'Then next month there's the Southern groups beat contest. But we

[1] This is how Colin Fletcher describes how his group found the Merseysound (*New Society, op. cit.*):

One evening the Tremeloes went to a Liverpool club to listen to a new and popular group. We were by then playing a combination of rock and rhythm and blues with a heavy pounding bass. We remarked that although the group on stage made less noise they had more power. Soon it was noticed that on stage there was a bass cabinet (amplifier) that was six feet high with two huge speakers. We realised that we needed one of those coffins. Two weeks later the bass amplifier was ready for trial. Even on the backing of soft chords there was a terrific pounding from the box. Immediately, the group started to adapt its regular numbers to accommodate an accentuated beat. Many groups had done this before the Tremeloes and within a year it was to become standard practice on Merseyside. As the bass note was bashed the drummer did the same and the whole line-up of guitars stamped and shouted. It was wild and basic. The sound so appealed to us that we, like others, built the music around the bass notes. The Tremeloes had achieved what came to be known as the Mersey beat.

could really do without them up here.' The cheers are wilder still.

Then it is the Mojos' turn. They have the same sound as the Escorts plus an organ. Their lead guitarist is a natural comic, and makes his guitar work as a banana-skin as well as an instrument. The couples are dancing again, most of them standing quite still facing each other, whilst they twitch and jerk their arms and heads. This seems to be partly an imitation of the rhythmic movements that guitarists unconsciously make as they are playing, and partly a simple solution of the problem of how to dance when it is too crowded to move. The bass guitarist of the Escorts is dancing with a girl in the audience, but no one is trying to make souvenirs out of his clothing.

At the end of the session, Bob Wooler reminds everyone about the lunchtime session the next day. 'I'm not encouraging you to skip work, but I'm sure you'll be able to leave half-an-hour early.' Outside in the street the Mojos are going into the pub. The twelve-year-olds are still there and still smoking. Down at the end of the road there is a sign in front of a side street: 'This is a Corporation play street.' It is quite empty.

The next day people are already queuing at 11.30. Some have left work much more than half-an-hour early, or are still on school holidays. But there are others who have nowhere else to go; Liverpool's unemployment figures this summer topped the 30,000 mark.

By the time the Cavern's full there are nearly five hundred people crammed in. It boasts that it is the only club in the country that has a live group at lunchtimes. Today the group is due to be Wayne Fontana and the Mindbenders, from Manchester, where the beat is almost as endemic as it is here. But they are late, and the audience, few of whom have brought anything to eat, listen with zealous enthusiasm to records made by local groups. When the Mindbenders arrive they agree to play for an extra half-hour to make up for being late. The group are indistinguishable from their Liverpool cousins. They have the

c

same brushed-forward hair, rounded-collar jackets and high-heeled boots. Wayne Fontana himself is a tough-looking seventeen-year-old, with a broad grin and a chirpy voice. The audience is soon clapping and singing with him, and it seems ridiculous that outside it is 1.30 in the afternoon, the rain is falling and people are going back to work in factories and offices. Nobody leaves before the session ends at 2.30. There is no screaming and no hysteria. In fact, there is very little sound at all as the audience emerge into a drab Liverpool afternoon.

Within six months, largely thanks to the Beatles, Merseybeat had become the most publicized craze in Britain's pop music history. It was evocative to a degree which was rare in any music of the city in which it had developed. The sound was tough, exciting and cheerful; the lyrics were usually optimistic;[1] and the groups and singers—at least while they were still in Liverpool—made no attempts to speak standard show-biz mid-Atlantic, or to dissociate themselves from their audiences. In the face of this, the popularity of Cliff Richard's much-publicized respectability, Presley's forced sexiness and Adam Faith's self-pity crumpled temporarily as easily as the Beverley Sisters did before Bill Haley.

The Town Hall, Berkhamsted, Hertfordshire: December, 1963

About a hundred people have come to this Friday night dance to hear one of the more popular local groups. Its members are all sub-eighteen-year-old apprentices in nearby Hemel Hempstead, a New Town whose brooding teenage population is the second largest, proportionately, in the country. With Merseybeat at its height, the town is sprouting groups in every factory and school. For the first time it has become economically

[1] A friend once remarked that the contribution which the Beatles have made to the improvement of lyrics is represented by the subtle, but not unimportant change from 'my darling' to 'my friend'.

possible to establish live locally-based music sessions as a regular part of teenage social life, and beat dances are being held in youth clubs, colleges, church halls and even open-air fêtes.

None of the five members of this group earns more than £10 a week in his regular job. If the group plays two evenings a week they can earn an extra four or five pounds each, once the manager and van driver have been paid their percentage. Consequently all their equipment, which is worth well over a thousand pounds, is on the H.P., usually over their dads' signatures. One of the guitars alone cost nearly £200.

The dance is slow in starting. The hall is local government green, and far too big for the number of people there. The group are playing popular beat numbers by the Searchers, the Swinging Blue Jeans, and Gerry and the Pacemakers. Their versions are passable, but in their stagey costumes (the singer has a shimmering red jacket) they seem just a shade too confident.

Up near the stage are a group of girls aged between twelve and fourteen. They arrived at the dance in frocks and flat shoes, carrying parcels that looked as if they'd been carefully hidden from their mothers. Twenty minutes later they emerged from the ladies' in bell-bottom trousers and thick make-up. Now they're leaning against the stage, and dancing and strutting in the singer's line of vision. They hope they'll get a ride in the van after the show. When the group is a better-known one, the girls at the front are older, subtler and usually more successful.

Scattered around the hall are clusters of boys in a curious aggressive stance: heads thrust forward, backs arched like longbows, arms folded in front of their bodies. They will gaze at the girls but rarely ask them to dance. Occasionally one will burst into rapid movement, then, dissatisfied, lope off to a new station on the floor. Simultaneously three or four others will rise up like a flock of birds and follow him.

In one corner, a group of rockers from a nearby village have linked arms and are doing high-kicks so energetically that you can hear the stamping of their motor-cycle boots above the music. The few country girls in their costumes and flared dresses are still doing the Twist, but that jerky dance from Merseyside has reached the South, and most of the girls are twitching their arms and heads in little groups of threes and fours. The boys, too, seem more willing to do this dance—which most people round here call the Shake or the Robot—than the more extravagant and potentially embarrassing movements of the Twist.

Towards the end of the dance the group proudly announce that they have written a song, and what's more have made a record of it. With broad smiles and considerable gusto they play it. It has guts and rhythm and a tune, but sounds like a compilation record of half-a-dozen well-known beat numbers. A few minues later, there's a burst of frenzied movement in one corner of the hall. A fight has begun and the attendants move in to stop the dance.

Some months after this, the dances at the Town Hall were stopped because of the frequency and violence of these fights. At about the same time, the group disbanded. They explained that there was so much competition in the pop scene at this time that they felt there was no room for anyone but full-time professionals.

The Marquee, Wardour Street, London: December, 1965

'Oooh, look at his boots,' the plump girl in the back row gasped. 'He must've copied them from me. He was always saying how much he liked them. He must've copied them.' On the stage were the Mark Leeman Five, their singer clad in extraordinary red pixie boots, and a 2½-inch-wide gold belt that rested dangerously low on his hips.

The Marquee has been described by the *Melody Maker* as 'the pop corner of the world'. It has something of a Tate Gallery quality about it, progressive and sometimes experimental, but with such a solid international reputation that groups who make their début there are almost assured of success. John Gee, the Secretary, has between twenty and thirty groups a week arriving for auditions. His choice from these seems to be infallible: Manfred Mann, the Yardbirds, the Action and a dozen other top-liners have all served their apprenticeships here.

Tonight is one of the rhythm and blues nights (there is jazz at the weekends and folk on Wednesdays), and the main group is the Alan Price Set. Alan Price was once the Animals' organist, until he left to form his own group. The Set have dispensed with guitars altogether and have a powerhouse front-line of organ, trumpet and two saxes. They play a mixture of pop and city blues in the style of coloured musicians from the prosperous Northern States of Michigan and Illinois. Their sound is rich and exciting, and by comparison the two-guitar line-up of the conventional beat group seems thin and repetitive.

There is very little dancing. Almost all the audience is seated round the stage, listening—in fact, *attending*. There are middle-aged married couples, and little mod girls eating the gentlest of snacks, milk and crisps. They are Alan Price fans. They are at the club every time he is here, yet they never scream, never try to touch him. Sitting next to one another are a woman in a spectacular floral trouser-suit, and a gentle, dark-haired girl who would look at home in a convent. One night there was a boy in the front row covered with history books, from which he was writing and illustrating an elaborate essay. There is here a unique mixture of genuine musical interest and incidental fashionability.

Up on the stage the group are playing more like a jazz band than a pop group: they are tight, controlled and always experimenting. The bass-player listens to and reflects the runs that Alan Price plays with his left hand; the front line some-times blows a solid block of sound, and sometimes complex phrases against one another; Price punctuates the lines he sings with jabbing organ chords. But unlike a jazz band, their musical inventiveness never swamps their scorching rhythm and blues beat. By the time this book is being read this sound could well have become a major trend in the Hit Parade.

(It did, for a short while, but was soon replaced by a rather different sort of live musical event.)

Alexandra Palace: May, 1967

At the door of Alexandra Palace, the Negro ticket-taker was grinning from ear to ear, saying: 'Let's having you tickets, thanking you.' A hipster stared at him, muttering: 'In the USA, Uncle Toms like you have been declared unconstitutional.'

Crates of banana scrapings were stacked at the door, denied entrance. Smoking banana scrapings is the very latest thing to take a psychedelic trip on. A passing Indian pornographer, who had tried it, said: 'It tastes like second-rate birdseed. Strictly a put-on. Those banana republics will stoop to anything to get rid of the stuff.'

The noise inside was deafening. Four beat groups went their separate ways, producing between them the Right Now Sound. Search-lights stabbed you in the eye, blinding you, and then winked off, blinding you even worse. Just inside the entrance a girl in a leotard writhed on a pedestal. Nearby, three people squatted cross-legged in a transparent plastic bubble marked 'Banana Be-In' and lit sparklers.

This rave-up was billed officially as the Fourteen-Hour Technicolor Dream and it was staged to raise money for the *International Times*, the hipster journal which is read from North Beach, California, to Piccadilly. The aim was to get 10,000 people to pay £1 apiece, and it looked at midnight as if at least 10,000 were there.

A huge screen hung from the balcony, on which was a coloured motion picture of what looked like protozoa, dividing. A koala-eyed girl stared mournfully at these squiggling, agglutinous shapes, saying: 'That's the story of my first marriage.' A couple danced dreamily to whichever of the four beat groups took their fancy, the girl saying to the boy: 'He says I'm the perfect oral contraceptive. What do you suppose that means?'

A foursome squatted on the floor, sharing wine and suryeying the passing throng, which was immensely colourful. The military uniforms looked like the retreat from Moscow. Weird-looking girls with even weirder-looking fellows. A very hip friend told me later the best way to survey the passing throng was flat on the floor, looking up.

The fragments of conversation were delicious: 'I like Tim Leary all right, but I can't stand the people around him.'—'But you're all supposed to love each other.' 'Yes, but we don't have to like each other.'

One boy is nuzzling a girl's dirty neck, while she's staring, rapt, at an abstract movie of red eating green—and very obscene it was. 'I'm told in the seventies we all get to be serious.' 'Really, we get turned off in the seventies? Whatever for?'

At the far end of the cavernous hall was an immense organ, shrouded in scaffolding, and here was the greatest crush of hipsters. Atop the organ, 40 ft up, a man in a purple shirt beckoned invitingly and suddenly a lot of other hipsters started climbing the scaffolding. 'I really believe they're beginning to break through,' remarked a girl. 'It's beginning to happen.' One man, halfway up the scaffolding, dangled like a monkey from one arm. Another, with a lighted candle in his teeth, climbed arm over arm. It all looked like something out of one of Cecil B. de Mille's orgy scenes—vaguely lascivious for no apparent reason.

But the organisers were worried. A loudspeaker blared: 'Please get down from the scaffolding. It's extremely dangerous.' First pleading, then threatening: 'If you don't get down from the scaffolding, the show will have to be stopped.' Then they turned the lights off, and that did it. Nobody likes to climb scaffolding in the dark.

'When he's alone, he can't connect,' said somebody. 'When he's with people, he connects all right, but he can't communicate.'[1]

So in clubs and dance-halls, London night-spots and Mersey-side back streets, fashions germinate and are sped across the country by scooter, excursion train and TV programme. A dance starts as an exercise in movement in a Northern cellar and ends up being mimicked on *Sunday Night at the London Palladium*. A girl from Notting Hill likes the way the Jamaicans' ankle-length dresses shimmer in their blue-beat dances and goes home and makes herself one out of a yard of towelling. A few months later they are being sold in the chain stores. The Rolling Stones record an obscure song by a Negro blues artist called Willie Dixon, and fairly authentic rhythm and blues in the shape of *Little Red Rooster* reaches the top of the Hit Parade.

[1] 'It Happens All The Time', John Crosby, *Observer*, 7 May, 1967.

Pop singers themselves often follow the same quick path from suburban coffee-bar to exclusive club. There are as few who jump straight in at the top as those who plod meticulously up the ladder. Sandie Shaw and Cilla Black were jostled by their close friends into mounting the local dance-hall stage and singing one number with the visiting group. The Rolling Stones made their first record only a few months after being discovered playing to overflow teenage audiences at an obscure rhythm and blues club in Richmond. Their story is typical of that of many contemporary groups.

Mick Jagger (the singer) and Keith Richard (lead guitar) met in 1961, whilst they were both studying in the Dartford area. They discovered they had common interests in music, and began listening to records together, an activity that soon developed into live music-making. Brian Jones (harmonica and guitar) met Keith and Mick in a Soho pub called the Bricklayer's Arms. Mick had come to the London School of Economics, Keith was an advertising designer, and Brian a destitute wanderer who had not long returned from tramping round the Continent. Their now notorious hair was already long and, becoming aware of certain shared preoccupations and ambitions, they began meeting regularly and working out their own versions of Muddy Waters, Chuck Berry and Bo Diddley numbers. They began visiting the rhythm and blues clubs in Ealing, and the Marquee in Oxford Street, where the resident group was led by Alexis Korner, then the most respected artist on the British rhythm and blues scene. Brian, Keith and Mick sent some tapes of their music to Alexis, who was sufficiently impressed to allow them to sit in occasionally at his sessions.

Playing with Alexis at this time was Charlie Watts, who was later to become the Stones' drummer. Charlie had a successful full-time job in an advertising agency, and as his friendship with the other Stones developed, his income helped to supplement their living allowance. The only other source of finance was the grant Mick received towards his studies at the L.S.E. Mick and Keith occasionally did odd jobs, but were frequently sacked because of their appearance. All of them at this time were becoming progressively more involved with their music, and more determined to put rhythm and blues on the popular music map. They were also, because of their reluctance to settle in any extra-musical careers, living off chips, stolen eggs, and occasional meat-pies from a stall by the Embankment.

Their original strategy was to infiltrate not the commercial pop scene but the traditional jazz scene. Many jazz clubs were losing members, and were in any case manned by older musicians. This latter fact was to prove a significant barrier to the Stones' progress, for the older jazz musicians shared not only the widespread prejudice against the Stones' appearance, but also a professional resentment against the efforts of these teenage novices to push their raucous music into the sanctums of jazz.

In spite of this opposition, the Rolling Stones were soon invited to stand in for Alexis Korner at the Marquee, and as a result were given a few single-night jobs at Ealing. Gradually they started to build up a following of young fans, and began to receive angry letters from parents because of their disreputable appearance. About this time Charlie Watts left Alexis to play with the Stones, and they recruited Bill Wyman as their bass player. It was now early in 1963. The Stones had decided that what they needed was a club of their own, a place where they could play regularly and become established.

They had heard that the rhythm and blues club at Richmond was shortly to lose its resident group, and that the manager, Gorgio Gomelsky, was anxious to find a replacement. The Stones volunteered their services at one pound per head per night. They were accepted, did their first job before an audience of about fifty, and went away with one pound ten shillings each. Three months later the hall was regularly packed with at least 400 people, and large queues were being turned away at the door.

So far the Stones' success had been due entirely to their own enthusiasm and efforts. They had practised diligently, listened obsessively, and had acquired the residency at Richmond through a combination of talent and determination. Now with the prospect of success suddenly very real, other figures started to cluster round the Stones. Gorgio Gomelsky made a film of their performances and invited journalists to see them at the club. One of these journalists, Peter Jones, introduced them to Andrew Loog Oldham, a young publicity man who had done some free-lance work for the Beatles. Andrew in turn invited Eric Easton, an experienced and well-known agent, to hear the Stones at Richmond. The agents saw that the Stones were sufficiently like the Beatles—and yet at the same time sufficiently different—to have a very real chance of achieving Hit Parade popularity. They expressed their enthusiasm by signing an exclusive contract with the Stones, and taking them for a recording session at a private studio. Some of the tapes that were made at that session, including one of a Chuck Berry composition, *Come On*, were sent to Decca, and after a number of re-recordings *Come On* was issued as the Stones' first record. It reached Number Twenty in the Hit Parade, and the Rolling Stones suddenly found themselves confronted by success. They were soon invited to go on tour with one of their idols, Bo Diddley, and went on to record a number that had been written by the Beatles.

The Stones' development, with its pattern of grass-roots origins, hard work and rapidly accelerating success, followed only then by the entry of guiding managerial hands, is typical, and hardly the sordid, commercial confidence trick which many sceptics see on any new group's début.

The 'ordinary kids'

'Dear Beatles,
    In some magazines they make you appear as if you're from everyday families. In others you appear sophisticated and conceited —the big-shot star type!
    Are you a regular snobby high-class group or are you one of us?
                                    A Fan (?)
                                    Harriet B., Brooklyn, N.Y.'[1]

[1] *Love Letters to the Beatles*, Anthony Blond, 1964.

The idols that the pop scene throws up in this way fall into three rough groups. First, the 'entertainers': the Ken Dodds, Frankie Vaughans, and Russ Conways. If they were film stars (and some of them are) the 'entertainers' would be advertised as 'suitable for the whole family'. But closer market research would probably show that it was chiefly the older half of the family that was satisfied with their suitability. Like the bulk of their audiences most of the entertainers are oldish (that is, by pop standards). Their weapons are melody, nostalgia and charm. Because of this, and because they have little to do with the urgent world of teenage fashion, I shall not be considering them any further here. They belong properly to light music, and have sidled into the pop scene like candy sellers at a sports meeting.

The second group are the 'musicians', whose appeal lies principally in the quality of their music, and for whom good looks and sharp clothes are irrelevant to success. Most of the 'musicians' are coloured: Wilson Pickett, Otis Redding and Ray Charles have been amongst the most popular. But because adherence to minority musical tastes is one of the ways in which the most modish of teenagers nervously protect their authority, some strange (and white) prodigies have occasionally appeared in this group. Carl Perkins was one of these. On his first time round in the early 'fifties Perkins was a popular young American rock'n'roll singer, who composed a number that Elvis was to make famous, called *Blue Suede Shoes*. In 1964 the mods revived classical rock'n'roll, and Carl Perkins, jelly-legged, balding, and clad in a knee-length tartan jacket, made a fantastic appearance on the TV programme, *Ready, Steady, Go*. His performance was electrifying, and so was the reception given it by the chic young audience, most of whose members can barely have been six years old when Carl Perkins made his name.

But the most widespread and pervasive of idols is the 'ordinary kid', so christened by Nicolas Walter.[1] The appeal of the 'ordinary kid' is broadly-based; frequently his intelligence,

[1] *New Society*, 28 February, 1963.

his industriousness, and even his musical talents are less than mediocre, and this has been the cause of some disquiet. (Though these talents have rarely been the sources of heroic appeal; the accidental gifts of beauty and aura seem to be much more important.) But he is always young, lithe, vigorous, and, in a gaunt way, physically attractive. He can be confident or confused, but never shy. His clothes and gestures may be discreet, but they are never clumsy. He is, by definition, successful, and by circumstance, rich. Yet for most of his career he is separated from his audience by only a few months in age and a few yards in space. He is, to use that shorthand expression that has become a substitute for working out what is probably a quite complex psychological relationship, somebody they can identify with. Less obscurely, he can communicate more completely with a young audience than can an older, maturer, more inhibited artist whose preoccupations in life are rather different.

It's curious, given the paramount status in the pop audience of the teenage girl, how very few of the 'ordinary kids' have been female. The fantasy sexual relationship between the girl fan and the male star can go a long way towards explaining this. But what is not clear is why the relationship between the *male* fan and his idols should be an almost exclusively mimetic one, involving a dialogue of styles and conventions that rules out male-fan/girl-idol groupings. Nor why there is no similar relationship between girl fans and girl singers; Sandie Shaw and Dusty Springfield, for instance, could hardly be said to be fashion-setters, or even fashion-followers. Yet the dress, gestures and overall persona of a young male singer are crucial in his relationship with his audience. He must present to them an image whose fashionable components are neither too far in front of their own—literally too 'way out'—nor too far behind. He is a crystallizer of styles rather than a setter; part-mirror, part-refinery for the audience's youthful self-image.

Up to about 1963, the 'ordinary kid' could have been defined at a more practical level. He was a Home Counties, ex-secondary-modern boy who lived on a council estate. He was Thomas Hicks, a merchant seaman from Bermondsey, who later became Tommy Steele;[1] he was Reginald Smith, alias Marty Wilde, a timber-hunker from Greenwich; he was Terence Nelhams, now Adam Faith, one-time film studio messenger-boy and member of the Rank Screen Services apprentices' skiffle group. Like their audience, most of these 'ordinary kids' were solidly working-class. (Though the customary signs that this was so were becoming fainter and fainter.) Middle-class teenagers, when they ventured into the pop scene at all, tended to play and listen to the more respectable fringe-forms of jazz and folk-music. Their publicly expressed opinion of pop was that it was boorish and un-musical—though one suspected that in private they were well aware of Luxembourg's position on their radio dial.

But since the Beatles and the groups that followed them began redecorating the pop scene with their refreshingly vital and unpretentious songs, the bulk of this prejudice has vanished. Partly this was a consequence of the infusion into beat music of the traditionally middlebrow influences of blues and folk. Partly, also, a result of the changing image of the singer, who was no longer the tortured adolescent prototype, with lamé jacket and padded flies, but aggressive, confident, and dis-armingly natural. There was also the underlying feeling amongst the young middle-class that what little indigenous culture they did have was stagnating, a feeling which was thrown into sharp relief by the upsurge of beat music in the wildernesses of working-class Lancashire:

[1] The stage-names that stars have thrust upon them are a revealing comment on the way in which impresarios imagine idols appeal to their audiences. All the early British teenage stars had names which were ingenious combinations of tough masculinity and homely up-rightness. As well as the ones mentioned above there were Lance Fortune, Billy Fury and Vince Eager. The first local rock groups, mostly self-named, stuck to the tough labels. You could find Panthers, Falcons and Tornadoes in most towns. But as the pop scene became more complex and the Mod replaced the Teddy Boy as the symbol of the time, the names of the proliferating number of groups necessarily became more sophisticated and distinctive. Amongst the more bizarre have been Tom Thumb and the Four Fingers, the Soul Agents, the Others, the Long and the Short, the Truth, the Who, and the Problems.

The three teenage children of a £12,000-a-year barrister I know, taken on a Mediterranean cruise, asked anxiously if, as first-class passengers, they would be banned from the second-class deck: they took it for granted that that was where the action would be. The old envy-syndrome, the Dickensian waif pressing pinched whey-face against the window of the bourgeois merchant's villa, teeming with plump offspring and plum pudding, has been reversed. To the young well-bred, locked up in their boarding schools and conventions, it is the high street scene, with its coffee houses, Wimpy bars, Bel-Ami multi-horned hi-fi juke-boxes and motor-scooter gregariousness, that. has the fun and drama.[1]

Currently both audiences and performers are representative of all classes, and fans seem to be able to 'identify' with stars whose backgrounds are quite different from their own. There is no evidence that Spencer Davis from Birmingham University, Paul Jones from Oxford, and Peter Asher (of Peter and Gordon), the surgeon's son, have a different type of follower to Stevie Winwood, from Great Barr Comprehensive, and Bill Wyman, the ex-office boy from Penge.

The teenagers who inhabit the pop scene are in fact in the happy position of being classless—or perhaps, more properly, in a class of their own. The Knightsbridge deb who models a dress and the Edgware mod who sells it are frequently indistinguishable. They may live and work in different areas, but you will find them in the same clubs in the evening and in the same shops at the weekend. But so ingrained is our belief that the marks of class *should* be visible, that it is still a source of surprise when East End accents issue from a face which looked more as if it was going to utter drawled Kensington.

The influx of Northern groups and singers into the pop scene (and for that matter of the Albert Finneys and Tom Courtenays into the theatre) has been one of the most striking examples of this process of class erosion. It has established Northern humour and speech habits as having a value in their own right, and not just as amusing deviations from the London

[1] Kenneth Allsop, 'Pop Goes Young Woodley' in *Twentieth Century*, Spring 1965.

norm. There were plenty of Northern pop singers before the Beatles—Gracie Fields and George Formby were internationally famous. But they sold their provincialness like bawdy postcards from a Blackpool souvenir shop, happy to act out the caricature that Southerners had drawn of them. For most of today's Northern singers—Cilla Black is a supreme example—regionalism is an incidental state, to be neither hidden nor exploited.

Plumage

One of the most powerful forces in the breaking down of class barriers in pop has been the Art Schools. Their tradition of bohemian classlessness and the growing interest in Pop Art and design amongst students have linked their preoccupations with those of the pop music world. The Art Schools are now turning out a high percentage of the personnel of Britain's top groups: the Beatles, the Animals, the Rolling Stones, the Kinks, the Who and the Yardbirds all have one-time art students amongst their members. And those that are more disposed to watch than play have been responsible for a good deal of the most original teenage dress fashion. The shaggy, brushed-forward hair that was the cause of so much of the Beatles' initial publicity had been commonplace in Art Schools for years. And after the Who had appeared on *Ready, Steady, Go* in their self-designed Pop Art clothes, roundels and Union Jacks (emblematic, not patriotic) were to be seen on T-shirts all over London.

Clothes, like singers, usually originate amongst the audience (or amongst the performers, who are close enough to the audience in every way for the two to be grouped together), and are only later taken up by the industry and thrown back at the teenagers, emasculated in form and increased a thousandfold in quantity. For those teenagers determined to keep one nervous step ahead of fashion this only serves to encourage even more complicated symbols of group differentiation.

A case history of fashion: the mod

The most extraordinary example of this sort of obsession was that phenomenon of fashion, the mod. The mod's chief observable characteristic was an excessive concern to keep up with and constantly change styles in clothes, dances and even food, and his conformity to his own type. If the rocker's point of reference was his membership of a face-to-face gang, then the mod's was adherence to the more impersonal mod 'image'. (Though rockers had an image, and mods would seldom be seen except in large groups.)

The concept wasn't new; there had always been fashions and fashionable youngsters. Sartorially, at least, the mods were the descendants of the Italian-suited youths of the early 'sixties. But here the continuity started to break down. Most of the mods were very young. There were older ones amongst them, sometimes converted rockers and graduated Italianates, but the vast majority were just out of—and in many cases still in— school, and were experiencing their first tastes of having any label at all. Again, unlike the dandies of the past, they were not products of the upper and middle classes. If mods did have a typical social background it was the new blocks of flats and housing estates in the cities and bigger towns. Their passionate concern with clothes was particularly apt in this setting. It emulated in an unsquare way their parents' search for social status by means of material possessions.

This obsession with clothes started unspectacularly enough; the Beatle-type clothes that have already been described were, in essence, mod. But for those who were temperamentally inclined to keep one conspicuous step ahead—or aside—from the teenage hordes, these soon became commonplace. Not only rockers, but the over-twenties were wearing Beatle jackets, a fact which ensured the mods' total and permanent antipathy. After this, for boy and munchkin (the delectable nick-name for girl mods) alike, the fashions changed at breakneck speed. The boys' round-collar jackets grew nominal lapels and big hunting pockets. The shaggy, brushed-forward hair was trimmed and parted down the middle, Oscar Wilde style.

Shirt collars went mad: they ranged in pattern from elaborate Paisley, through Black Watch tartan to bright orange polka-dot; they became at one extreme so high that it became difficult to move one's head about, and at the other vanished away to a thin mandarin band fastened with a cuff-link. The girls, many of whom designed and made their own clothes, were drabber but no less inventive than their male counterparts. Those ankle-length skirts, which could be made up out of a couple of yards of old curtain, vanished almost as quickly as they appeared. Not many girls would venture out in these skirts in the daytime, but for a couple of months they were prescribed wear for the dance-halls. It was fascinating how the mods instinctively seemed to be able to match up their clothes and dances: to see twenty or so munchkins in their long skirts and Juliette Greco hair-styles, doing their jerky, pushing dances like sea-horses swimming against the waves, was weirdly attractive. These thirteen-, fourteen-, fifteen-year-old girls had somehow contrived to look graceful.

As the hot weather approached in the summer of 1964, dress styles changed even more radically. The mods were at least sensible enough to realize that they didn't have to sacrifice comfort in order to be fashionable. The boys started to dispense with their anoraks, which they had worn when riding those other symbols of mod extroversion, scooters. (Scooters became as decorative as clothes, with fox-tails tied on the handlebars and saddle, and dozens of useless chrome lights on frames at the front.) The girls' skirts became shorter until they stopped a few inches below the knee, and then changed abruptly to ski-pants.

By the summer the drift towards identity of the sexes that had been apparent ever since the mods had become a recognizable sub-group, had reached its inevitable conclusion: both sexes looked identical. At times this amounted to near-transvestism. Mod girls had always been inclined to masculinity in their fashions, and not only did they copy the boys' clothes and crop their hair short, but the whole pattern of their mannerisms and behaviour seemed to be an elaborate structure designed to disguise their femininity. They had their own flat-footed walk, and rather than dance with boys they preferred other mod girls with whom they had worked out complicated routines. Some of this can be explained by the fact that many of the teenage girls who were attracted to the mod image were naturally rather plain. Discovering a fashion which made a virtue out of interesting ordinariness, they were able to cash in on something that had previously made them socially unsuccessful. They may not have got more boy-friends this way, but at least they got more stares. And there was no longer a premium on femininity; far from attracting the boys, excessive delicacy seemed to put them off. (In the mod boy, extravagant effeminacy seemed to be confined to a very small minority. Even these were apparently heterosexual, and it was probably sheer outrageousness that made them wear lipstick and eye make-up, sling-back shoes, and occasionally leather skirts.) Curiously enough—for a lot that was new in the pop world had seemed to be a reaction against American softness and sentimentality—the final image was almost a parody of the healthy young American beach-boy. Both sexes had closely cropped hair, T-shirts with initials or the names of American high-spots sewn on them, jeans or pale-coloured slacks, and canvas shoes. The light-weight clothes suited the energetic, bouncing dances that were in vogue. The mods of summer '64 jived like their elder brothers did ten years before, and revived rock'n'roll artists like Bill Haley and Carl Perkins. With original fads becoming more and more difficult to devise, the past provided a rich store of ideas.

In the end, mod girls' fashions became so popular that they ceased to be the prerogative of that brittle, image-conscious minority. High fashion, having failed to beat them, joined them, and in the winter of 1965, almost every young woman who bothered at all about clothes was wearing P.V.C. coats, short skirts and lacy stockings.

To satisfy the mods' needs for conspicuousness, novelty and group security, it was vital that fashions progressed. But where each new fashion originated is something it is impossible to pinpoint. Crazes could change overnight, literally, and it was easy to be fanciful and imagine a coterie of arch-mods somewhere in the wilderness between Shaftesbury Avenue and

Oxford Street, deciding what the next plumage was to be. Where the fashions certainly did not originate, as any comparison between what was being worn in the streets and what was on display in the shop windows would reveal, was inside the fashion houses. Indeed, the rag trade had great difficulty in many cases in keeping up with the changes. It did, of course, cash in on each craze after it had got under way (usually with considerable gain, for the average mod spent £5 to £8 a week on clothes), and in the provinces was genuinely responsible for introducing new fashions (with slogans like 'Latest in the West End'). They were helped in this by the more ambitious out-of-town mods ('Ticket Boys') who would go up to London for a long Saturday night, and bring back the news of the latest fashions.

The focus of the mod boy's clothing world was Carnaby Street, a small side-street near Oxford Circus. In this street there were, at the height of the mod craze, eight men's clothing shops, most of them owned by the same man. It was almost impossible to move along Carnaby Street on a Saturday morning, so large were the crowds of young men gazing in the windows. (Which they seemed to do more than go inside. Deciding what to buy when they went home, perhaps?) In fact, a special policeman was drafted to Carnaby Street with what appeared to be the sole task of keeping the crowds moving so that everyone could have a look.

In spite of the almost mythological status which Carnaby Street achieved, even its young designers were not responsible for *creating* more than a handful of the mainstream of mod fashions. The designers were interpreters rather than innovators. The original fashions started right at the grass roots, copied from singers, picked up by teenagers in their evening haunts, and knocked up next day, perhaps on the girl-friend's sewing-machine. The long dresses and pork-pie hats that were popular for a while came from Jamaica via the blue-beat clubs. The high-collared shirts from the Star Club, Hamburg, where the Beatles and most of the other well-known beat groups had gained their early musical experience. The I.T.V. pop programme, *Ready, Steady, Go*, also imposed a weekly cycle on

the already rapid mutations of clothes and dances. 'The Weekend Begins Here', it announced amid a flurry of animated pop
art. With teenage announcers, and mod dancers imported from
London clubs, it never failed to be influential.

But the most interesting, if not the most important, source of
mod fashions were the *faces*. A face was a top mod, who took
the whole thing very seriously indeed, felt he had some sort of
responsibility to the movement in the matter of creating or
choosing new clothes and dances, but felt also a little disgruntled at the fact that he could never maintain his unique-
ness, and would always be copied not only by his friends, but
by twelve-year-olds in towns a hundred miles away. One
unusually articulate mod felt very strongly about this:

> There's quite a crisis in the real mod world about all these
> fashions and dances leaking out so quickly. The pace of change
> has been hotted up so much—a clothes fashion and a dance
> fashion could last for about three months before, but now they're
> being imitated by all these little 'Chods' (anybody who's not a
> mod) from the countryside.
>
> You see it's all to do with loneliness really. It's because they
> come from such really *deadly* homes; you can't *imagine* what
> their home life is like. Parents who they don't *know*. And the
> world that their parents represent is such a *drag*, all this *work*
> you know; knitting and television and everything—and they live
> in the suburbs in endless rows of council flats and playgrounds
> and in 15 minutes they can get to London, you know; clubs and
> coffee-bars. The commercialists are catering for them.[1]

For all their mayfly superficiality, the mods struck crippling
blows at both the dull uniformity of 'men's wear' and the
upper middle class monopoly of smartness. The sixteen-year-
old working-class boy and girl of today are unrecognizable if
one compares them with their shabby, servile equivalents of
fifteen years ago. Inverting James Laver's thesis that the bour-
geoisie are always the innovators of fashion, *their* clothes are

[1] Interview in *Cherwell*, 23 June, 1964.

now the prototypes for West End modes. Mary Quant, who stands with one white boot in the teenage market and the other in an increasingly similar *haute couture*, finds much of the inspiration for her designs by watching teenagers in the streets and dance-halls of South-East London.

If popular means 'from the people', fashions today are popular. Starting from a Royal College of Art drawing-board, a pile of old Edwardian dresses in the Portobello Road or a rhythm and blues group's working clothes, they move through the TV pop shows and the West End boutiques to end up finally—and almost simultaneously—in Chanel and the provincial Marks and Spencers.

This pattern of the sudden appearance of a new idea, its fast diffusion through the modish teenage audience, a brief moment of stability and then another sudden change, is understandable when we consider the social function of dress. Clothes are signals about the wearer's personality. They are one of the ways we declare the sort of person we are, and recognize the broad social personalities of others. Thus they can fulfil either an expressive or a communicative function, depending on whether we define ourselves as wearers or observers. But for the insecure teenage under-achiever this duality can be a source of tension: he wants to express himself, yet at the same time he would like to accept membership of a category of young people, defined, in part at least, by a certain mode of dress. I don't think it would be too far-fetched to see in this conflict between the desire to be a unique individual and the need to share in the security of a group, the source of the restless cycle of teenage fashions.

Plumage: *July 1967*

The one constant thing that seems to dominate the young during this decade is a sense of style. Not for three-quarters of a century—perhaps since the age of the Aesthetes—has British youth been so obsessed with the outward appearance of things. And it is not for nothing that the 'pop' phenomenon has taken root in England faster than anywhere else in Europe. Pop singers and groups who rely almost exclusively on innovation, presentation and quick-change appeal for survival have set the prime examples for the younger generation of stylistic means of coming to terms with themselves and society.

Paul McCartney goes to India for a holiday and, the next we know, 'digs' from Hampstead to Earls Court are littered with batik-patterned fabrics, silver bells, incense burners, brass trays and joss sticks. The New Vaudeville Band produces a couple of hits called *Winchester Cathedral* and *Finchley Central* in an Al Bowlly, megaphone style, and a 'thirties revival is confirmed. Richard and Jagger are sentenced in connection with drugs, and the long-pressing problem of narcotics immediately becomes a cause célèbre in the daily press, with *The Times* taking a stand for law reforms. But do the pop groups set the styles, or is it actually the other way around?

Chris Farlowe cut a disc not so long ago which indicates the predicament dolly-birds and teeny-boppers must find themselves in. On a label appropriately titled *Immediate Records*[1] he shouts to an accompanying sitar

> *You're out of time, my baby*
> *my poor old-fashioned baby.*
> *You're obsolete, my baby*
> *my poor old-fashioned baby.*

The lyrics repeat insistently, against a background of Indian sounds:

> *Baby, baby, baby, you're out of time,*

adding the admonishment,

> '*You thought you were a clever girl*
> *giving up the social whirl.*
> *You can't come back and be the first in line . . .*
> *You don't know what's going on*
> *you've been away far too long . . .*

Here is the style-syndrome of the Swinging generation.

An era preoccupied with style is an era of mannerisms, and mannerisms depend on the mannered, the change or novelty for

[1] Who print on the jackets of all their 45s: 'Proud to be part of the industry of human happiness'!

its own sake, the quickly digested ready-made appearance of something hot off the fashion line. Thus Art Nouveau design can be stencilled on coffee-bar posters, put on pop record sleeves, made into wall patterns, dress fabrics, furnishings, or even turn up as set designs for television. But since each fad spreads so quickly, the ability to sustain interest or excitement is low, and the style must change—a condition capitalized by gear shops. 'Granny Takes a Trip' has gone through at least three switches of outdoor décor since it opened: the entire shop-front including window, door and woodwork, was first covered with splashy Art Nouveau swirls, then a giant face of Jean Harlow, and most recently with an American Indian's head—arch-symbol of the West Coast Hippies.

If Art Nouveau, itself a mannered style, was the first of these easily adaptable fashions to be applied to every form of pop culture in the 'sixties, 'thirties-style now seems to be in. Blue-glass coffee tables, tubular steel furniture, smoky-mirrored walls. Almost over-night, pre-Raphaelite shifts of lace and frills have been exchanged for beaded dresses and transparent chiffons. The movie poster of Garbo or Dietrich has replaced the sinuous Mucha lady. And a sophisticated pop artist like Roy Lichtenstein actually produces a theatre poster which parodies himself parodying 'thirties-style. Lichtenstein's poster sells for £6 at Austin Reed; the movie poster can be bought for as little as thirty bob. At throwaway prices, everyone can afford the latest Camp, and there will be something new coming along next month.

In clothes, men have had a rougher time staying with fast changes, but recently they've been catching up. Regency velvets and ruffled fronts, after all, were expensive items for a short-lived fashion. But a shop in the Chelsea Antique Market has neatly solved the male sartorial problem at a price level to fit any hipster pocket. Old demob suits were bought up, re-cut and sold for £8; Second World War sailor trousers, dyed at home in bright mauve, orange or purple, sell for £2. They also make an Indian collarless batik shirt that reaches to the knees and costs sixty-five shillings; perfect for an evening with Ravi Shankar.

'I was Lord Kitchener's Valet', which is just off Carnaby Street and has a branch at the Antique Supermarket, sells its stock of old, heretofore-unwanted military uniforms faster than they can be replaced, along with policemen's capes and military hats. A Grenadier Guards coat worn with blue jeans was the rage in June, but already that's been replaced with kitsch-coloured Carnaby Street jackets, printed in huge, gaudy floral patterns.

An older more conservative generation who bought their suits by post from the Army and Navy Stores year after year, knowing they could be certain of always getting the same style and quality, might look askance at all this quick-change fashion. But examine the economics of the situation: the prices of Savile Rowe or even Regent Street are well beyond the income of an overtaxed young Englishman, and Bond Street has priced itself out of the range of the ordinary secretary-typist. So they have found clothes that are cheap enough, gay enough, wearable enough, just, at a price that allows them not only to discard when the style changes, but also actively to take part in the fashion change itself.

Art-forms in an age of stylistic mannerism become a way of life and tend to infiltrate every level of design. The gear shops themselves have, in their décor, typography and window display, as well as in their merchandise, turned into pace-setters. The polished steel hoardings of 'Bazaar', the aluminium walls of 'Count Down', the psychedelic exterior of 'Dandie Fashions', and the dark, deep-blue plasticised atmosphere of 'Way In' (at Harrods of all places) become extensions, not only of the fine art of the times, but of the clothes on the racks, as well as the record albums being sold at the next counter. After all, it isn't by accident that the gear shops flip their décor as often as they do the pop tunes blaring out the newest hits as you try on the latest 'drag'. In fact, the entire appearance of Carnaby Street changes fortnightly, its exterior décors attempting to outdo each other with bizarre, outlandish ideas which often make it difficult to find the clothes under all the window-dressing.

This insistent and continuous need for change—what one writer has labelled 'the tradition of the new'—was foreshadowed by the pop artists as long as a decade ago and is reflected in the kind of expendable art-products currently being shown in West End galleries. How prophetic Andy Warhol looks now, with his system of a picture factory, where hundreds of copies of the same image are silk-screened to meet demand, and where the image changes to meet the fashion. The graphic designers, television designers, record-sleeve artists, lay-out men on the glossies, and ad-men are quick to get the point and have managed effectively and ingeniously to absorb what the fine art boys have done. Any week, TV's *Top of the Pops* will cue you in as to what is the latest thing in painting and sculpture: last month it was Minimal art, this month Kinetic and Optical, dovetailing with the new psyche-delic fashion.

This conscious awareness of style in the 'sixties, this preoccupa-tion with the way things look, has come to mean that more people are more aware than ever before of their visual environment. And, before one knocks it, it is as well to remember that it represents an up-grading of taste, a keener awareness of the things around us as they infiltrate our lives and our art. One now has total freedom to make one's own choices; to select, to create, to borrow or reshape exactly what one wishes and without any predeter-mined restrictions. Who can censure a generation so full of energy, enthusiasm, inventiveness and individuality, a generation that has made a style for itself and its own time?[1]

Display

When we look at dances we see similar patterns, both in origins and in significance. The Ska began as a Jamaican folk-dance and was brought to this country by West Indian immigrants; the Twist (however commercially dubious the way it finally *reached* its enormous public) evolved in the Harlem dance clubs of the 'thirties. Killer Joe Piro, a Manhattan dance-instructor, once explained how he helped to infiltrate the American upper classes with this sensuous, traditional ghetto movement:

> All that hip movement. . . . It's got new names, but you know they were doing that at the Savoy Ballroom in Harlem when I was 17. Remember that boogie-woogie shuffle stuff Cab Calloway used to do? Harlem was doing the Twist 30 years ago and didn't know it. Negroes and teenagers, that's where the new dances come from. . . . I watch them and steal a lot of their stuff. Some-times I have to clean it up. A little 16 year old can get away with wiggling her hips while her hands are on the back of her head. It's cute. But when I teach it to a 40 year old divorcee I'll keep her hands a little bit lower, just over her shoulders.[2]

[1] Mario Amaya, 'The Style of the Sixties', in *Spectator*, 14 July, 1967.
[2] *Saturday Evening Post*, 27 March, 1965.

The Twist was an interesting development in a process that has been going on in popular dance since the early 'fifties, and which perhaps throws some light on the function that dancing fulfils for teenagers. Ever since the days of jitterbugging the contact between partners has been diminishing. When jiving came in with rock'n'roll, the dancers simply clasped hands as they shook their hips and threw each other in the air. In the Twist there was no contact at all. The boy and girl stood nominally facing one another as they gyrated, but were quite often not dancing 'with' one another; to move opposite a partner was an agreeable alternative to solo dancing, which was (and still is) regarded as mildly eccentric. It was also, for the boys, a prelude to an easy pick-up.

But the Twist, and most of the dances that have followed it, is principally for dancing by oneself. The beat of rock'n'roll and rhythm and blues is there to be danced to, and is usually effective enough to get most people moving, if only in their chairs. The sensuality of dancing, which once lay in the tender touch of cheek upon cheek has now been transferred to the movements of the dance itself. (In much the same way as has happened with the lively teenage dancers of West Africa, who would never dream of allowing embracing and grappling to get in the way of their energetic displays.) Consequently, girls are no longer regarded as wallflowers if they do not dance with boys, and many of them—to judge by their performances on the floor—seem to prefer dancing with one or more of their own sex. Even the boys are beginning to do this, and though I have seen them thrown out of a number of the more strictly-marshalled dance halls because of it, more and more are indulging in patterns of intensely self-involved solitary movement.

Dancing is now a courtship display rather than an act of courtship. The principal interest of the girls (and of the more fashion-conscious boys) is not so much in attracting their opposite numbers as in competing against each other. So, as the contact between boy and girl has diminished, the intricacy of the most fashionable dances has increased. They are now far more subtle than in the days of jiving, and the violent leaps and kicks have been replaced by complicated movements of the feet and head. (I have seen professional ballet dancers look clumsy whilst trying to imitate the foot-twirling and swaying of some London mods. The latter, too, have spent many hours practising in front of mirrors.) But there can be a monotony and an inflexibility in even the most elaborate of these movements. Dancers will repeat the same complex step over and over again, as if it were their one secret trick.

Unlike clothes, dances cannot be bought: they have to be learned. Consequently, class differences are more evident in dances, and the most fashionable steps from the West End clubs reach a wider public only in very rudimentary forms. By the time they have reached the upper middle classes they are almost unrecognizable. But the changes which they undergo on their journey between Soho and the county seats are a clue to the importance which working-class teenagers attach to dancing. At the Hunt Ball the debs will make the appropriate movements, most probably fail completely to co-ordinate them, and laugh the whole thing off. In the discothèques the mods will be dancing brilliantly, but in deadly earnest. Dancing is one of their few means of self-expression, and a new dance confidently performed is not only a personal achievement but a visible sign of clan membership.

Dancing: September, 1966

The revolution in British pop music and dance is generally seen as having its roots in United States popular culture. People are not generally aware of the particular influence, in this revolution, of a music and dance form (called the ska) which is prevalent among the Jamaican lower classes. To examine this influence is a useful corrective to the usual studies of minority groups. These studies nearly always assume that cultural contact is a one-way process. They conceive of a dominant culture (the host community) and a minority culture (the immigrant or minority group); and, from then on, only the problems of the minority group in adjusting to the host society's culture are seen as worth analysing. But cultural contact and social assimilation are never one-way.

Ska is what the music and dance are called in Jamaica; in

Britain, in its undiluted form, it is the 'blue-beat'. The ska is a unified form—i.e., it consists of a unique, easily recognizable rhythm which is identified with a special kind of dance. This kind of form has a long tradition in both African and European culture: in Europe, as early as 1300, unified forms like the ductia and the estampies; more recently, the waltz, the tango, the fox-trot. The early period of rock-and-roll lacked unified music and dance forms, until Chubby Checker introduced the twist.

The ska was created around 1961 by the lumpen proletariat and urban lower classes of Jamaica. The music which accompanies the dance consists almost entirely of a monotonous, pulsating and compulsive rhythm. In Jamaica this is usually emphasized by the guttural grunts and groans of the dancers, who act like an exhausted person gasping for breath. The melody and lyrics are always secondary, serving mainly as a framework for the rhythm. The dance, accordingly, is of more interest.

It is usually performed in couples but there is little co-ordination or sexual specialization in any of the movements. These tend to be very flexible. The dancer stands with his feet slightly apart and his body bent from the waist, as in a bow. The body is then straightened and bowed to the rhythm of the tune, the neck plunging in and out like a turkey. There are several hand movements, the most characteristic being a muscular jerk convulsing the whole body. It is carried out with the arms held out in front of the dancer, slightly bent at the elbows. The movements of the legs tend to vary with each performer.

The ska began to make its impact on British popular culture less than three years after it had emerged from the shantytowns of western Kingston.

At first it was heard and danced mainly in the discothèques and nightclubs of Soho and Brixton, most of which had formerly specialized in rhythm and blues, jazz, and other aspects of the predominantly negro elements of American popular art. In 1964, however, Millie, a Jamaican teenager, produced a ska version of an old American pop song called *Lollipop*. It was an immediate success and, retitled as the blue-beat, the ska soon became popular among the young people in Britain.

After its heyday in 1964 the blue-beat seemed to go the way of so many other fads in modern popular arts. But though the more obvious elements of the rhythm have declined, the accompanying movements have become the basis of British popular dance, and the modified ska is now referred to by various other names such as the 'shake' and the 'jerk'.

The diffusion of the ska among the British has brought about several changes. The first is the greater muscular play given to various parts of the body, and to the body as a whole, while dancing. This is a conception of dancing wholly alien to the west European, and particularly to the Anglo-Saxon, dance tradition. The traditional posture has been to keep the torso fairly straight, at times even rigid, with movements restricted to the legs and the shoulders. Second, spontaneity has become increasingly important in dancing: improvised muscular contortions, especially from the waist upwards, are carried out within a loosely defined pattern. Third, there is the disappearance of stereotyped conceptions of masculinity and femininity. In dances like the veleta, the military two-step and almost any other of the Old-Time forms, there was always a strong emphasis on the masculinity and aggressiveness of the male partner who was expected to lead the woman, and the coyness and delicacy of the female who followed. Now the female dances in excatly the same fashion as her male partner and in many instances appears to be even more aggressive.

Finally, the communal framework of British popular dance has shifted rapidly from 'organic solidarity' to that of 'mechanical solidarity'. The traditional west European popular dance forms required some specialisation among the dancers. This type of organic solidarity—each dancer performing a specialized role, harmonizing with the rest towards a given aesthetic goal—received its classic exposition in the ballet. New dance forms are 'mechanical' in that they consist of each individual performing all the possible moves or roles required by the dance. Any solidarity among the dancers derives from the sameness of every movement.

The ska or blue-beat largely derives from the dancing and music inside the Pocomania cult. There was a slight revival of secular music and dance at the beginning of this century. Revived slave dances and songs soon merged with musical influences from Latin America and other parts of the New World to produce the mento—a kind of Jamaican version of the Trinidadian calypso. By the mid-1940s, however, Jamaica was swamped by popular American music. But it is significant that the acceptance of this new American influence was highly selective. The most popular songs in the island were almost always rhythm and blues, especially among the predominantly negroid lower classes.

The lack of a genuinely Jamaican music and dance form was strongly felt by the working class and lumpen proletariat. Towards the end of the 1950s, they turned to the native Pocomania cult and borrowed its music and dance. When combined with the negro American rhythm and blues, this became the ska. I have already explained how the ska arrived in Britain. Rhythm and blues was always popular among a small group of the British public, almost from the moment it became widespread in the United States. Over the past four years or so, it has got much more popular. Much of the supposed originality of the Beatles and the Rolling Stones and the mass of their imitators is a direct borrowing from the pure rhythm and blues. Such cross-pollination is not uncommon. In its transmogrification into the shake, the jerk and other similar forms, the ska reveals its impact not only on Britain, but also on the United States where it was vigorously promoted by the Jamaican government and tourist board. These dance forms came to Britain via America.

So much for the ska's background and process of diffusion; but the crucial question still unanswered is: why have these alien patterns of recreation established themselves in Britain?

Till recently, British society has been one of the most remarkable experiments in living. It had a culture that was unusual among western societies both for its homogeneity and stability, and for the complexity and sophistication of its internal mechanisms of change, adaptation and social control. As long as the underlying pattern of conflict within the society remained the same, these highly complex mechanisms remained efficient in their resolution of whatever new forms of conflict emerged. But when the underlying pattern of conflict in a society changes, as it has in Britain, two things follow: (a) new mechanisms of adaptation must be developed; and (b) the very complexity and sophistication of the traditional techniques come in the way of resolving the new types of conflict.

One of the basic factors in the rock'n'roll revolution was the shift by the entertainment industry toward the youth sector of the population. Youth-organisation emphasizes virility, action, sensationalism, speed and violence. The violence factor, more than any other, makes the youth-oriented, hedonistic ethic unacceptable to the traditional system in Britain. This system is conspicuous for its compromise, conciliation and avoidance, at whatever cost, of any overt form of violence. When overt violence does occur, it is either considered as deviant and treated as such, or canalised into socially acceptable forms of behaviour.

Today a large part of the population thinks that a certain type of violence and aggression is both necessary and desirable. But the only response of British society has been to treat this behaviour as merely another form of the traditional pattern of deviance. So a self-fulfilling process occurs. The alienated youth population identifies its incipient hedonism with the traditional forms of deviance. It has no other way to express its violence, and almost all other aspects of its hedonistic ethic are frustrated by the still largely Protestant-oriented older group. The young people realize that whatever they do will be interpreted, in any event, as simply another form of deviance. Only this can explain the sheer anarchy and meaningless iconoclasm of the smashing up of seaside resorts, destroying public telephones, wrecking trains or desecrating cathedrals.

Similar patterns of youth violence are observable in the United States—for example, the Newport and Fort Lauderdale riots. But with its more flexible and heterogenous culture, and its fuller recognition (if not acceptance) of the nature of such forms of non-deviant violence, the United States has, to some extent, developed the necessary adaptive cultural technique for dealing with it. There are the beat movement; certain aspects of the civil rights and other political movements; the emergence of new recreational forms and literary and cinema productions specially oriented to youth; and the significant reorientation of the attitudes and values of the older group to meet the demands of the younger sector.

With one exception, British culture has failed to provide the institutional techniques to meet the new situation. The exception is music and dance. This is one of the most significant means of expressing not only the violence, but all other aspects of the hedonistic ethic. As in all other spheres of traditional culture, the music and dance of Britain could not satisfy the demands of its new, alienated youth group. Popular negro music and dance like the ska is essentially the recreational pattern of an alienated people, developed to express the rage, the anger, the violence and the vitalism of a sub-culture which, for various historical reasons, is basically hedonistic in orientation.

It was what the youth of Britain lacked.[1]

[1] Orlando Patterson, 'The Dance Invasion' in *New Society*, 15 September, 1966.

There is little doubt that the majority of fashions in idols, clothes and dances originate inside the teenage audience. There is little doubt, too, that they help to satisfy certain needs which this audience has for change and security. (The provision of these two combined is, after all, what fashion is all about.) To this extent they can be said to be popular fashions. But they are frequently obsessive, and when we return to music itself, often only superficially rewarding. In the next two chapters we shall examine the extent to which this is due to pop music's involvement with the mass media.

Another case-history: the Hippy

1   In America

See you at the freak-out. Over on McDougal Street a group called The Fugs ('amphetamine opera and sex rock'n'roll' played on Indian finger cymbals, buffalo-hide drum, harmonica, Brillo box and fartophone) are serenading their audience with:

> *What are you gonna do*
> *After the orgy?*
> *I wanna read Blake with you*
> *After the orgy.*

If the music and the message really grab you (so long, Beatles, Rolling Stones and other old-timey entertainers), you will find in Tenth Street's Peace Eye Book Store . . *The Fugs' Song Book*. . . . The Fugs propagate Group Grope, the new American together-ness: 'freak-beans from their collective existence, the Body Poetry Formula.' It's terrifically psychedelic.

New York, you spoil one, there's so much to do, so much to see. Let's get this show on the road. Call in at Andy Warhol's Balloon Farm to hear the Velvet Underground, otherwise the Exploding Plastic Inevitable, combining piano, violin, guitars and tape machine blasting musique concrete. Really blows the mind. On the screen behind the stage floats a Warholocaust of huge film images, dream faces of men and girls beatifically stoned on LSD. As the amplified electronic feedback, wilfully distorted, builds up to uncountable decibels, smaller screens beside the stage are bombarded from projectors with swirling, bilious colours and patterns. Simultaneously, on the stage the Cher-like girl chanteuse with tambourine and a male dancer jab at the spectators with mauve strobe lights.

Of course the New Thing—what you've got coming to you, you may feel, if you hang around the discothèques too long—is not peculiar to downtown Manhattan, an indigenous tribal ceremony. It is already being exported. The freak-out (a telescoping of teach-in and cook-out: the lesson is peace and mysticism, but, confusingly, the provender is stimulated psychotic disturbance) is at large on these shores. London has its pop-art disc cellars, flickering with kaleidoscopic glares and cartoon films. The Who have for ages been smashing their instruments in autodestructive happenings. The Creation embellish their act by flagellating guitar strings with fiddle bow and wet potato, and by flinging luminous paint around. Even in far-off Glamorgan, the Electric Poets articulate plastic pop with a kit including an electric razor. And, of course, in both Britain and America, with equal trendy promiscuity, psychedelic is a label slapped on to mod kits, verse, ear-rings, cinema, jazz and, for all I know, aerosol after-shave. Suspicion sets in at the Balloon Farm to start with. It used to be a Polish social club, this hangar-sized ballroom, pounded by polka-ing boots. What Mr Warhol puts on there now is quite an elegant piece of Theatre of the Absurd, a ruthlessly rehearsed happening. But there are disquieting reminders of primordial Saturday nights at the Locarno: the blue-and-pink spotlights on the waltzing tulle as the saxes mooed Deep Purple and the globe of mirrors revolved under the rafters, winking its rainbow romance. Should not a psychedelic voyage be more than eyeballs-aching? Any sign of Nirvana to starboard?

All those people with cans of underground movies under their arms and the lapel buttons saying 'Sterilize L.B.J.'—you won't find it easy to wring from them the admission that they haven't exactly themselves crunched a cube. Even Dr Timothy Leary, evicted from the Harvard faculty because of his drug samplings, rather coyly elects the initials L.S.D. to stand for his League for Spiritual Discovery. At the Village Theatre on Second Avenue, Dr Leary, hunkered bare-foot and in mahatma-white, holds his Death of the Mind 'public worship service', a reading from The Tibetan Book of the Dead and, you bet, some home movies in which the earth-bound, materialistic intellectual is portrayed struggling to be free, even of the flesh of women. . . .

D

On the other hand, this is not the unanimous attitude down in St Mark's Place and around First Avenue. Certainly God is very Groovy at present. Incense drifts from many a store-front shrine, with the tinkle of temple bells, Ravi Shankar records, strains of raga, and the chant 'Hare Krishna, Hare Rama, Hare Hare'. Swami Bhaktivedanta holds his class in Kirtan meditation three times a week in an East Village shop, and the Swami says firmly no LSD, marijuana, alcohol or illicit sex in his gang. His disciples accept his rule of 'Turn Off, Sing Out, Fall In'. This is bound to be bewildering to the psychedelic apprentice, since such a guru of the New Bohemia as Allen Ginsberg pays public homage to Krishnamurti, a Hindu holy man, and also to marijuana. Fortunately, there is the Kerista, a much more all-purpose paradisiacal cult, which offers 'Utopia Tomorrow for Swingers', and recommends communal living and loving.

Multisexuality is, anyway, in harmony with what can most handily be described as the multi-media movement. If time hangs heavy on your hands in the East Village between evensong and matins, no problem. Secret cinema at the Film-Makers' Cinematheque: say Tom McDonough's *12-12-42*. There's *The Golden Screw*, a folk-rock musical, at the Theatre Genesis. Browse through the Psychedelic Golden Goodies at the House of Oldies on Bleeker Street. Buy a sweatshirt branded TURN ON, TUNE IN, DROP OUT or MAKE LOVE NOT WAR, a sampler of the 'sixties. Check out some of the newer pop freak groups, such as? and the Mysterians, or Count Five (their current hit is *Psychotic Reaction*), or Love (a choice of name that strikes a popular chord, for Tuli Kupferberg of the Fugs has redesigned the American flag so that the stars spell LOVE, and carried it at the Love Pageant Rally in Tompkins Square on the day California outlawed L.S.D.) Invest in a half-finished low-budget 35 mm. movie entitled *Chafed Elbows*, 'about a man who marries his mother, they go on welfare and it all breaks into a rock and roll musical'— that's the advertisement for a backer. See what the Radical Underground in Sound and Light is putting on at the Gate: Jazz-Midnight-Images, Two Improvisational Events, Spin-Art (Create Your Own Abstract), A Happying at the Infestival (love-joy fest and kinetic lighting).

There are, too, the art exhibitions of life-sized plaster people, giant comic strips and canvases bulging with lavatory seats or melted type-writers, quivering sculptings in plexiglass and neon tube, decorations in vinyl, scrapyard junk and flashing bulbs, erotic robots, plugged-in magnesium mobiles gyrating like lighthouses, suspended metal cutlery sets for monsters, cybernetic columns remote-controlled by computers—the commedia dell' arte for an overheated culture, all the latest in engineering art, laser beams instead of brushes and electronic brainstorms instead of canvases. Why have your own nervous breakdown? Buy it at the box office. Dr Leary has declared: 'Only psychotics, flipped-out saints and psychedelics know how to pray. You have to be out of your mind to pray.' The Fugs' mood music does fit in.

Cher, of Sonny and Cher, belonging to a slightly earlier phase of pop, has said rather starchily of psychedelic music: 'It will replace nothing but suicide,' and one American paper heard in the Velvet Underground atonal echoes of 'Berlin in the decadent 'thirties'.

Calculated chaos and the destruction of barriers is the announced aim of much mixed-media endeavour but, of course, once trip-hammers and acted-out sadism get into the theatre, and once induced schizophrenia is accepted as a condition of LSD ecstasy, the guide-lines grow hazy. Dr Leary says: 'I had to create a new religion because society is in an insane asylum but we're too close to see the lunacy.' Likewise, there may be increasing difficulty in distinguishing the boundaries of the larger freak-out into which the Village voyeurs go when the show is over.[1]

2   In Britain

In music, a potent if not always admitted influence on several 'psychedelic' pop groups has been the work of Cornelius Cardew. He collaborated with Karlheinz Stockhausen in 1957–60 to produce *Carre*, a forty-minute work for four orchestras, four choirs, and four conductors. His own *Treatise*, performed at the Commonwealth Institute last April, can last up to four hours; a one-hour version was recently broadcast by the BBC. Recordings of collective improvisations by Cardew and four other performers, using prepared piano, two cellos, guitar, saxophone, two transistor radios, and other equipment, have been issued under the Satie-esque titles *Later During a Flaming Riviera Sunset* and

[1] Kenneth Allsop, 'Turn On, Tune In, Drop Out' in *Spectator*, 9 December, 1966.

After Rapidly Circling the Plaza. Cardew has performed at Ufo and the Round House, but finds the atmosphere uncongenial, even though he does not intend his music to be 'listened to academically', but to 'produce a kind of high'.

Cardew's influence is most apparent, to my ear, in the playing of the Pink Floyd, who went professional in February and recently issued their first L.P., *The Piper at the Gates of Dawn.* Their earlier single, *Arnold Layne*, was banned by Radio London because it was about a clothes fetishist. 'Psychedelic' pop groups use amplifiers of ear-splitting power; feedback in place of a melodic line; various electronic gadgets, such as reverberation units, fuzzboxes, and oscillators; electronic generators to set up a powerful back-ground hum; and unorthodox tunings (Eric Clapton, guitarist with the Cream, tunes his top string a minor third higher, as if it were on a banjo). Some 'Eastern influence' is creeping in: the Beatles use a sitar on the *Within You Without You* track of *Sgt Pepper*, and the Move, a car-wrecking group from Birmingham, who on one occasion nearly burnt down the Marquee, have made similar experiments. There are, in fact, constant efforts to discover new musical and extra-musical effects. The Pink Floyd have tried playing guitars with cigarette lighters. Roy Wood, the Move's lead guitarist, sometimes uses a violin bow. The Soft Machine have experimented with free-form music and poetry reading; the *Melody Maker* calls them 'loud, naïve, and entertaining' (17 June). The group known as Tomorrow wear imposing masks and costumes for their mimes of death, resurrection, and fertility; their disc, *My White Bicycle*, suffers from the exclusion of this visual element. The eponymous leader of the Crazy (sometimes, Incredible) World of Arthur Brown is the Underground's eccentric and clown. With grotesquely painted face, he leaps from side to side or leans far out from the stage on his immensely long legs, haranguing his audience in a blues monologue, wailing, screaming, cajoling, wisecracking, and finally setting his headdress on fire. Recently arrested for possessing dangerous drugs, Arthur Brown has just invented 'pornographic pop', in a show with the Exploding Galaxy. . . .

The only original art form associated with the Underground is the light-show, in which static or moving abstract coloured images are projected on screens, musicians, and dancers. Stroboscopes project flickering lights, which are supposed to synchronize with the brain's alpha rhythms and can produce epileptic seizures in predisposed subjects. Kinetic art machines (snow and flame machines) throw gliding or dancing patterns on ceiling, floor, and elsewhere, so that the observer feels he is floating in light. The painter Mark Boyle, a lecturer at Hornsey College of Art, was the pioneer of this art form in Britain, and there are now at least twenty-three separate light-show specialists from whom equipment and operators may be hired. Much use is made of hollow slides, into which coloured oils and other fluids ('evolving jelly') are injected. Dermott Harvey, a biochemist, has invented a machine to inject colours in a way that allows precise control over the amount of fluid and the point at which it enters the slide; subsequent movements are unpredictable, and no effect can ever be recaptured exactly. A pop group called the Social Deviants have their own light-show, and Jack Braclin, a photographer, makes light-shows the central feature of his Happening 44 club in Gerrard Street, Soho.

Several light-shows are always to be seen on Friday nights at the Ufo club. Those who enjoy Ufo speak warmly of the empathy and non-verbal communication attained there with people of like mind. Verbal communication is scarcely possible, so loud is the music. The visitor sees a collection of charming but withdrawn individuals, smiling vaguely at friends, jerked at times by the music's rhythms, but ultimately quite self-sufficient and self-absorbed as each intently explores his private world and savours his private visions. Ufo in macrocosm was seen at the Alexandra Palace Technicolour Dream, which was many people's introduction to a new and virtually contentless form of entertainment; an imitation Ufo for older people was the Electric Garden, which outraged Underground die-hards by selling alcohol and otherwise fostering 'bad vibrations', but has now been 'given over to the scene' and renamed Middle Earth.

Both Ufo and special events are advertised by means of vivid posters, in which the styles of Alphonse Mucha and, to a lesser extent, Aubrey Beardsley are tempered with astrological, Aztec, and North American Indian influences. Lettering is pure Mabel Lucie Attwell, but in any case tends to be kept to a minimum, since the aim is to communicate intuitively rather than verbally. These posters seem to work better than the analogous neo-Art-Nouveau designs by Wes Wilson for Bill Graham's rock-and-roll dances and light-shows at the Fillmore Auditorium in Haight-Ashbury. They are the products of 'Hapshash and the Coloured

Coat': two young men, that is, called Michael English and Nigel
Waymouth, who have developed their special style because 'almost
none of the advertising done by the older generation works for our
generation'. They try, not to sell or persuade, but to convey a
feeling, a mood, a state of mind. Their poster advertising Tomorrow's *My White Bicycle* disc was rejected by E.M.I. because it
showed naked breasts; their second attempt, plastered with con-
cealed phallic symbols, was accepted. They have also designed
record sleeves and shop-fronts, but the shop-fronts they did for
Michael Rainey's 'Hung on You' boutique in Cale Street, Chelsea—a shop patronized by the Beatles and the Rolling Stones—
had to be taken down when other shopkeepers complained that it
'lowered the tone of the neighbourhood'. Some advertising
agencies have offered them work; some are starting to imitate
them.

Waymouth is associated with another boutique, 'Granny Takes
a Trip', on King's Road. Nearby is 'Dandie Fashions', run by
Neil Winterbotham and John Crittle (the latter recently charged
with possessing dangerous drugs). All three shops are distinguished by the youth and engaging unprofessionalism of their
proprietors and designers. In an effort to make young men's
clothes gentle and unaggressive, they have done away with
shoulder padding. Jackets are close-fitting; trousers, tight round
the thigh. These are nostalgic styles, in some respects harking
back to the pre-Raphaelites, but mingling influences quite
eclectically. Long, double-breasted overcoats or Indian-style
tunics do service as jackets; at 'Hung on You' the most popular
garment last spring was a quilted, high buttoned jacket in the
style of Mao Tse-tung, called 'The Great Leap Forward'. Shirts,
often tailor-made in satin, have mandarin or high, pointed collars
and ruffles down the front. Ties are not worn, but a loosely tied
scarf often hangs outside the shirt front. Bright colours are
mandatory: pastel shades or floral patterns for summer suits,
swirling greens and blues or tiny floral patterns for shirts. Winterbotham favours rich, shiny, crushed velvet; Rainey, gabardine;
Waymouth, whatever he can get hold of that is colourful and
primitive. Not only Carnaby Street has been influenced by these
leaders of underground fashion: Scandinavian boutiques are
already displaying signs announcing 'THE HUNG ON YOU STYLE',
and Dandie Fashions plan to open a branch in the U.S.A. As the
mass producers close in, copy, and undercut, Chelsea begins to

advance into fresh territory; flowing, tight-sleeved robes, in Arabian and Aztec styles, worn over wide satin trousers. These are now being designed for 1968.

The Clothes-Makers are not alone in having a head for business. The Underground as a whole is a paying concern, with bank accounts, an efficient accountant (Michael Henshaw), and a penchant for forming companies as a protection against 'hustlers': the spivs of the Underground, who make their 'bread' from exploiting other people's ideas. The *International Times* is owned by Lovebooks Ltd (registered June 1965) whose directors are Hopkins, Miles, Henshaw, Haynes, Moore and McGrath. Art dealer John Dunbar, singer Peter Asher, and bookseller Christopher Hill are, with Miles, directors of Indica Books Ltd (registered September 1966). Hopkins and Henshaw are directors of U.F.O. Club Ltd (registered May 1967). And Miles and Henshaw are directors of E.S.P. Disk Ltd, registered last February to produce tape recorders and tapes. Each company has a nominal capital of £100. There are ideas for a television consortium that would apply for a licence in five years' time. There is talk of at least one pirate radio station, and of an Underground Arts Council to subsidise artists and writers. As publicists and organizers, the Underground businessmen are nothing if not flexible. Even *I.T.* is not intended to remain a newspaper for ever. Already several special issues have been put out in fly-sheet form; and tapes, video-tapes, and sandwich boards may serve *I.T.*'s purpose in the future. The Underground suspects our printed culture is doomed, and does not mind giving it a kick or two on the way down. It takes its communications theory from Marshall McLuhan, just as it quotes Wilhelm Reich and Eric Berne on social and psychological matters. But it is hard to judge how far these thinkers have been digested.[1]

[1] Peter Fryer, 'A Map of the Underground' in *Encounter*, October 1967.

5   Sources of fashion: the operators*

Both T.V. channels now run weekly programmes in which popular records are played to teenagers and judged. While the music is performed, the cameras linger savagely over the faces of the audience. What a bottomless chasm of vacuity they reveal! The huge faces, bloated with cheap confectionery and smeared with chain-store make-up, the open, sagging mouths and glazed eyes, the hands mindlessly drumming in time to the music, the broken stiletto heels, the shoddy, stereotyped, 'with-it' clothes: here apparently, is a collective portrait of a generation enslaved by a commercial machine. Leaving a T.V. studio recently, I stumbled into the exodus from one of these sessions. How pathetic and listless they seemed: young girls, hardly any more than 16, dressed as adults and already lined up as fodder for exploitation. Their eyes came to life when one of their grotesque idols—scarcely older then they—made a brief appearance, before a man in a camel-hair coat hustled him into a car. Behind this image of 'youth', there are, evidently, some shrewd older folk at work.[1]

Paul Johnson has already been chastised enough[2] for the article from which this extract is taken, which must have been one of the most spiteful, snobbish and ill-informed pieces ever to be published in a reputable and supposedly socialist journal. But in his more sober final sentence there is an element of truth: the men behind the 'grotesque idols'—the managers, the agents, the P.R.O.s, the disc jockeys—are almost all much older than

* December, 1965.

[1] 'The Menace of Beatlism' in the *New Statesman*, 28 February, 1964.
[2] See George Melly's unanswerable reply in the *New Statesman*, 7 March, 1964.

their clients. Because of this, their motives for continuing in the pop scene are bound to be different from those of an eighteen-year-old singer.

But the operators' motives, as well as being ultimately impossible to plumb, are irrelevant in assessing the degree to which they condition pop music. Whether they are in the business to make a quick fortune, or to 'give the public what it wants', they help shape the pop scene in ways which are not wholly related to these aims. When a baby-talking disc jockey announces to seven million listeners that 'this is going to be *the* big sound of 1966' it makes precious little difference to the effect whether or not he believes this. Not that we can ever be sure of what the effect is: the interaction between the media and their capricious audience is too complex for anyone to say 'this singer was successful because of the way he was presented on television' or 'this song was killed by over-plugging'. But there is a pattern in the treatment which pop music receives from TV, radio and the music press. Certain styles of presentation and ways of criticizing (or not criticizing) recur again and again. It does not seem unreasonable to assume that this is neither accidental nor without influence.

This chapter, then, is concerned with the character of pop's presentation, both live and by the mass media, and the way that this reinforces (or counteracts) tendencies which are already evident in the conventions of the music and the behaviour of the audience.

What a bottomless chasm of vacuity they reveal

Of all the TV and radio pop programmes, Rediffusion's *Ready, Steady, Go!* on Friday evenings has, deservedly, the highest reputation. *R.S.G.*'s success has been due entirely to two unique features: live performances and a carefully chosen teenage audience. *R.S.G.* was the first television show to risk live appearances by top recording artists, and it was an initiative of which those shows that have kept to miming must be very jealous. It demolished finally the widespread myth that most singers could only make an acceptable noise with the help of recording-studio tricks. (A few groups have been conspicuously absent since *R.S.G.* went live, but the reasons for this may be quite unconnected.) The majority—and the Animals and Manfred Mann, in particular—have proved what anyone who has seen them perform in clubs or dance-halls knew all along: that they are far more exciting playing freely to a responsive audience (with all the loss of echo and effects that this may mean) than attempting to move their mouths in time with a record, which, after a hundred identical plays, has lost all meaning for them.

Ready, Steady, Go's choice of music is wide and progressive, and it never confines itself to the safe favourites of *Juke Box Jury* and *Thank Your Lucky Stars* (though it does tend to pander to London modishness).

It has presented distinguished blues artists like John Lee Hooker and Jesse Fuller, and folk-singers like Buffy St Marie, Paul Simon, and Donovan when the latter was still a scruffy lad just up from St. Ives. And one memorable Friday—it must be the only occasion on record when the dancing stopped completely—Paul Jones of the Manfred Mann group was allowed to sing *With God on Our Side*, Bob Dylan's biting anti-war song that the B.B.C. had unofficially banned.

R.S.G.'s audience are mostly teenagers from London clubs, and to be admitted to the programme they have to pass a short dancing audition. The producers presumably feel that the subsequent loss of spontaneity is a small price to pay for the stylish, fast-moving character which they give the programme. For, in spite of a tendency to become giggly and exhibitionist when they see the cameras near them, they are mostly very good dancers indeed. (Like the faithful troupe of shouters who follow Geno Washington's Ram Jam Band, they are more extensions of the groups than members of an audience.) In fact, for anyone who finds live musical performances as exciting to watch as they are to listen to, *R.S.G.* is a visual goldmine: cameras swooping back and forth like robot jivers, tangled black leads from the guitars, and Pop Art décor. Admittedly, all of these serve to exaggerate the excitement of the music. But they are more an integral part of pop than the equivalent accoutrements at a serious concert are of classical music.

R.S.G. is much talked about by teenagers, particularly outside London, where it is one of the few channels through which knowledge of the latest fashions can be obtained: the viewers know where those dancers are chosen from. But it is precisely in an arrogant awareness of this fashionable reputation that the programme's main weakness lies. The hostess, Cathy McGowan, for all her disarming artlessness and powder-room chatter, is constantly dictating what is, is not, and will be 'in'. There was once a ritual in which one of the visiting stars would wander round the audience and pick out the girl he would most like to go out with. Not that she ever *got* a date, of course. Her rewards were usually a peck on the cheek and a free L.P. How one wished that, just once, the star or his luckless choice would refuse to collaborate in this embarrassing and rather cruel charade.

There could be no programme more different from *Ready, Steady, Go!* than B.B.C.'s *Juke Box Jury*, and no programme which has done more to damage the image of pop music amongst uncommitted viewers. A panel of four judges—a typical combination would be two starlets, a comedian and a disc jockey—listen to a collection of the latest releases. Their function, as they are constantly reminded by the chairman, David Jacobs, is simply to predict whether each record will be a 'Hit' or a 'Miss'—that is, whether or not it will enter the Top Twenty. As they listen to the records, the reaction cameras peer at the faces of the studio audience (for success-clues for the panel?).

When about 30 seconds of each record have been played (this is assumed to be enough to judge it on), the members of the panel give their comments. The comedian makes a joke about the title, the disc jockey explains how he had lunch with the recording manager, and the starlet says how lovely it would be 'after the party's over, and you're left alone with someone special'. David Jacobs hovers in the background, soothing occasional quarrels between the judges, assuring the viewers that so-and-so didn't *really* mean that he hated the last record, and, as if to deter the panel from ever voting and recording a 'miss', randomly producing from behind a screen the singer of the record on which they've just voted.

If there is anything more pointless than a programme predicting the future popularity of records, it is one laced with 'discussion' and occurrences like these. But *Juke Box Jury*'s approach is typical. On almost every occasion when pop is discussed in the mass media there is the same reluctance to criticize, the same all-pervading cosiness. Bowing before mass culture's general edict that the customer is always right, the purveyors of pop music do not acknowledge that there is such a thing as a bad record; there is only a record that is liked by less people. As substitutes for standards, there are the Hit Parade, *Juke Box Jury*'s predictions and Radio London's 'Climber of the Week', all measures of actual or probable statistical success.

One would have thought that the pop music papers, being one stage removed from the actual music, could have afforded to ignore this formula. But their record reviews show the same enthusiastic neutrality (though the fact that their main advertising revenue comes from record companies no doubt has a great deal to do with this). Spicy—though usually fairly accurate —descriptions of the records invariably collapse into prophecies about their fate.

The following are reviews chosen at random from four of the main music papers in this country:

Julie Rogers—LIKE A CHILD

Another big ballad from Julie. This time there's no matrimonial issues involved, only a pleasant big ballad with Julie in vocal form *par excellence*. It has a certain grow-on-you quality, and although there's more adult than teen appeal here this should be a successful follow-up. Similar in conception to her last, though not lyric-wise. Flip is a smooth version of the Ruby and the Romantics hit. Gentle and smooth, but a certain hit flavour about it.

Record Mirror

Peter and Gordon—I GO TO PIECES

Peter and Gordon, on Columbia, have a slowish lilter with

I Go to Pieces. The now familiar sound of the two well-blended voices is unchanged and, although the song itself is pleasant enough, it lacks sufficient individuality to register an immediate impact. This, despite the polished overall sound, will make five or six spins necessary before the disc makes any progress.

Pop Weekly

Roy Orbison—PRETTY PAPER

A slow Country and Western ballad from Orbison this time out, but with a definite Christmas flavour and no doubt just right to corner his now-expected quota of the market.

Tune's very easy to hold and the wistful theme of the lyric suits Orbison perfectly. A well-made recording from every angle, and one that's a certainty for the upper Ten again.

Disc

Freddie Lennon—THAT'S MY LIFE

Immense curiosity value here, if only because Freddie is John Lennon's father. He's spent much of his life at sea, and this nostalgic monologue is very autobiographical.

Opens with the effect of the ocean breaking on the shore, then Freddie recites his tale in that infectious accent we've come to expect from the Liverpudlians.

Slowly swaying rhythm, with strings and background humming, and the group singing the title phrase.

Corny, but he's got the name to carry it!

New Musical Express

It seems remarkable that any journalist could be so gullible as to take Freddie Lennon's sad parasitism seriously. Yet the rule is that all records shall receive the diamond stylus treatment; the harshest comments you will find are remarks like 'this . . . will make five or six spins necessary before the disc makes any progress'.

The same attitudes prevail on the pirate radio stations. Ever since Radio Caroline first sailed out from Harwich in the spring of 1964 these pop freebooters have been the subject of violent controversy. Two successive Postmasters-General have vituperated against them, and the Council of Europe at

Strasbourg has searched for a loophole in international law that would make even the high seas forbidden to them. Using the sledgehammer, all-or-nothing arguments that have become the distressing commonplace of arguments about pop culture, the protagonists have taken up their positions. The authorities would like the pirates sunk because they have beaten the system; the Performing Rights Society would like them summonsed because, with the exception of Caroline, none of the stations pays royalties on the records it uses; many educators, fearful for the cultural life of a nation listening to round-the-clock pop, would no doubt like them municipalized, and turned over to educational broadcasts. The pirates protest that listeners must have a free choice and that, with 20 million a day preferring their static-ridden stations to the clarity of the B.B.C., there can't be that much wrong with them.

Scarcely anywhere in this welter of argument has there been a mention of the music itself, and the quality of its presentation by the pirate stations. Both sides see pop music as a commodity, though one sees it as beyond reproach and the other beyond improvement. It would have been interesting to see the difference in the arguments if the pirates had felt that the most profitable material for broadcasting was Pinter plays and Britten operas.

Nevertheless, if one believes that there is some worth in modern pop music, there is a great deal of criticism that can be levelled against the pirates: not because they play solid pop, but because of the *way* they play it. It is difficult to convey the tone of their approach in words. . . . On all of them there are the same burbling, insanely cheerful voices, stringing together the same words, grunts and noises to fill in time between the same records: 'Audible wallpaper', one journalist called it.

Good Afternoon! Ladies and gentlemen, guys and gals and little ones, a big hello and welcome to you. This is the Double Dee show with yours truly Mike Lennox swinging until three. Once again I seem to be in great big Bubbling-over-type mood and I hope that some of it will rub off on to you and make your day just a little bit, ah, brighter. . . .

But for young housewives, trapped at home by sinks and

cots, this supermarket approach seems to be overpowering. When Dave Cash, one of Radio London's most popular D.J.s, went into hospital because of a kidney complaint, he received 5,000 get-well letters in three days. And when Keith Skues referred to himself as 'Cardboard Shoes' on Radio Caroline, Caroline House was swamped for days afterwards by carefully constructed cardboard footwear. One suspects that the response this chance remark elicited is not so different from the response the music produces after it has undergone the relentless arti-ficial-sunlight-and-Musak treatment from the D.J.s.

Ready, Steady, Go! gone and the Pirates sunk: October, 1967

John Snagge, it's said, still goes white and silent when the new Radio 1 is mentioned; but everyone else at Portland Place seems to be taking its arrival pretty coolly. 'Good morning, sir,' say the commissionaires to the shaggy youths in camelskins as they lope into Broadcasting House; 'Good night, sir, not very good weather is it?' as they lope out. And it would take more than Mike Lennox dressed in his black silk shirt, blue striped trousers and green embroidered carpet to distract the drinkers in the B.B.C. Club. Emperor Rosko, then, in what he calls his 'everyday clothes', that's to say, shirtless in yellow trousers? I doubt it.

After all, B.B.C. radio once before had a reputation for eccentricity and iconoclasm. The fly boys of the 'thirties did, of course, grow old and go right and respectable (Snagge, presumably, with them): but it would be odd if no legacy of tolerance had remained. So stories of flower people being spat at in the gentlemen's wash-room are to be distrusted. They, and similar scurrilities, are presumably being put about by defeated pirates. And indeed, watching and hearing the Lennox beneath the carpet, polite, personable, thoughtful, quietly articulate, the kind of promising young man one might find in any profession, from hotel manage-ment to merchant banking—watching him in the B.B.C. Club, one felt that he could easily be absorbed into the B.B.C. hierarchy. Not portentous enough for a Snagge, perhaps, too mellow for an Alvar Lidell; but good, adaptable, corporation material. And why not? After all, Cliff Michelmore started as a disc jockey, and look where he is now.

It's a mistake to accept the *Mirror* image uncritically, and see disc jockeys as a simple compound of gaudy troubadour and raving social revolutionary: they are, in fact, quick-witted, ambitious, rather cynical young men, anxious (like the Snagge or Michelmore generation) to secure themselves a decent wage, a reasonably secure future and a little passing acclaim by exploiting shifting public taste. If the demand for pop recedes and that for something new increases, as seems to be happening in the U.S.A., we can expect the survivors among the Lennoxes to adapt easily enough. As for dress—well, most only wear camelhides and carpets because they feel it's expected of them. What the B.B.C. has done, in fact, is recruit a new batch of young announcers.

I say 'survivors', because the corporation has given short-term contracts to more disc jockeys than it really needs—29 in all—and has made it clear that a weeding-out will take place soon. Every programme on Radio 1 is apparently being taped for post-mortems in senior offices. The B.B.C. has deliberately created an insecurity which, it presumably hopes, will root out any slackness or sleepiness. And, of course, with the virtual extinction of piracy, there are no parallel opportunities for employment. Altogether, the disc jockeys are likely to prove as malleable as the B.B.C. wishes.

Like the established church, it is staging a largely phoney 'revolution': absorbing a modicum of would-be dissent, expanding its ideological tenets a little, trying to persuade everyone that the change goes deeper than it does. For Radio 1 is only the belated rationalization of a Light Programme that had resisted natural change and remained too close to the popular taste of the 'forties.

The change would not seem so abrupt if normal development had taken place. The apparent novelty of Radio 1 is simply a measure of how far the Light Programme had lost touch, not just with a new generation of teeny-boppers, but with the nation's housewives. Indeed, the pirates succeeded precisely because they won a vast following of disaffected housewifery: it was this that attracted their advertisers.

And even now Radio 1 exists for only seven or eight hours a day. It shares the rest of its time on the air with Radio 2. Admittedly, this often means that Radio 2 is getting 1-like programmes; but it also means that curiously traditional patches occur in the evening—*The Clitheroe Kid, Any Questions, Friday Night is Music Night.* The B.B.C. is, in effect, conceding its audiences to television between 7.30 and 10.00: and, having done so, will it get them back afterwards for what looks like being the closest to genuine innovation the Radio 1 'revolution' is going to produce? That is a regular Monday to Friday programme called *Late Night Extra*.

It is the old *Roundabout* plus something. As well as records and chatter and anecdotes from the compère (or disc jockey) it offers short interviews, live and 'canned', brief pieces by radio 'columnists', confrontation and disagreement, intermittent phone calls on any subject from members of the public, linking programmes with stations in America, breaks for news flashes from a mobile radio car attached to the programme. If a newsmaker arrives at, say, Prestwick, the D.J. might call him and interview him live by telephone. 'Nothing will be static, I'm not committing myself to any regular pattern', says David Carter, the programme's organizer. 'It all depends on what's available, and who's doing the programme.'

Lennox was 'doing' a dummy run of it on Friday, bouncing and swaying to the records he introduced while tweedy B.B.C. traditionalists watched from the control room. They played a tape of a cheerful Catholic priest who described how he brewed beer, 'threepence a pint for double the strength', and gave it to his bishop: then 'here's a B.B.C. Top 20 tune'; then a spoof phone call from a Mr Williams who told Lennox, a Canadian from Radio London, that he was taking English people's jobs and exploiting the N.H.S. 'There must be very many people who like me', says Lennox blandly. 'Sticks and stones may break my bones but . . .' He added something about moving in the grooving here on Radio Wonderful. 'May I call you dear hearts and gentle people? I hope I'm not being too familiar, but I like to establish a mood between you and me.' And so on, through a news item about the Albert Hall being burned down and an interview with a Liverpudlian who knew the Beatles ('I would have thought George would be the last one to get mixed up with all this . . . this philosophy and thinking about life') to 'a very special, personalized goodnight, and hope you'll join me next Friday night. 'Bye.' And with that, Lennox stalked out of the studio, scratched his carpet, abruptly dropped the mid-atlantic honey and the professional D.J. manner, and said worriedly that he thought it had gone badly.

Well, no one seemed to do much better when Radio 1 began operation early on Saturday morning. It began with Tony Blackburn shouting 'Let's get out of bed and twist the old kneecaps

a bit', went on to Duncan Johnson and Keith Skues playing more
records; and so to the manic Michael Pasternak, or, as he likes
to be called, Emperor Rosko. He presumably merits listening
practice: the B.B.C., which has given him an embarrassingly ful-
some build-up, thinks so, and so does the *Express*, which has
given him his own weekly column. As it was, my transistor radio
shook and bounced with the effort of making him intelligible.

When he speaks, he speaks fast and loud; but he mouths as
much as he speaks. 'Ga, ga, ga, ga,' he seemed to say, sometimes
interrupting the record to say it. 'The keeter with the teeter your
leader now . . . it's moody, moody, a googy goo . . . all right, baby,
that's blubby blub, don't wear it out and you can sing along if
you want to . . . that's it, hippies, we going to congregate here
next week, it's your number 1 station, hiya team population . . .'
The meaning doesn't seem to matter much: Rosko's style is
strictly non-verbal, rather a matter of tribal verve and hubbub,
presumably comprehensible to initiates, set to a background of
electric guitars. He sends the journalist scampering for the
fashionable quotation from McLuhan—and, indeed, so does the
D.J. phenomenon in general.

How is it that a disc jockey often gets more fan mail than the
singers he is presenting? The impresario more than the leading
man? Perhaps it's because listeners regard him as a bridge between
the actual and the dream. He moves among Springfields and
Lennons, remote unknowable meteors, and is touched by their
glamour; but he speaks to you, person to person, in down-to-earth
chummy language. Indeed, the competent D.J. welcomes technical
faults and poorly synchronized records because they give him a
chance for chitchat, apologetic or truculent, that increases the
informality and 'humanizes' a programme. The programme that
goes wrong may be going right for him.

He exploits a double appeal, then, a combination of proximity
and distance. He also speaks very fast, cracks rather lumpen
jokes ('James Bond's shoes were hurting him, and they asked him
what size he took, and he said, oh, oh, seven'), uses the only
classless accent available in English, verbally winks at his listeners
from time to time, asking them how they're feeling, giving them
his love, telling them when he drinks a glass of water or lights a
cigarette; and (very important, it seems) stops introducing a
record only when a good few bars of it have been played, and
starts introducing the next before that one ends.

This is what has been going on (and on and on) on Radio 1
since Saturday morning. 'That's Nancy Sinatra and it's going to
be a real hit . . . what a record it is! It was nice, nice, thankyou
fellows . . . that was an incredible beautiful record, wasn't it? . . .'
Congratulations abound. Disc jockeys congratulate the singers
and, more obliquely, themselves and their colleagues: 'Kilroy was
here. Who was Kilroy? A four-mile stretch of the East Lancashire
Road disguised as Keith Skues.' Every now and then jingles are
played, congratulating everyone and everything: 'Radio 1 is
wonderful—it's a blast.' By the time Twiggy had appeared and
been told that no photographer had ever done her beauty justice,
one felt that commercials would be superfluous on Radio 1. Most
of it is one long substitute.

But is all this much more than Radio Luxembourg, not to
mention every small-town radio station in America, has been
offering for years anyway?

Rosko apart, there was little in the first days of Radio 1, little but
the youth of some of the voices, that represented an advance on *Pick
of the Pops*, which Alan Freeman presented on Sunday and had
been presenting for nearly six years. The real novelty of Radio 1
is simply that dear old *Pick of the Pops* goes on, as it were, for
several hours a day. You can't really claim, with the *Sunday
Mirror*, that the B.B.C. has suddenly become 'a flower-powered
swinging chick in a micro-skirt'. The newspaper build-up the
new service received, surely unparalleled in the history of British
sound radio, has, one suspects, come to embarrass its organizers.

Wild talk creates impossibly wild expectations. No wonder the
Express's jury of 'children of showbiz stars' decided that Radio 1
was more miss than hit. 'If this is the best, then I am not looking
forward to the worst,' said Bernard Braden's daughter; and
another added, significantly, that it might have been better if
everything had been relayed from a boat on the Serpentine.

The truth is that the pirates succeeded largely because they
had the glamour of illegality about them: something the B.B.C.
obviously scorns. Yet its task is to stop the demand for the
restoration of the pirates. It has until the next election to achieve
this: the Conservatives are still committed to 'free' radio and, if
they find any exploitable dissatisfaction with the B.B.C., any
quantity of lost boppers among the new voters, might be persuaded
to do away with Radio 1 in favour of a commercial network. The
parallel with the B.B.C. local radio experiment is close. A

Conservative administration could well hand that over, too. Alternatively, a sound equivalent of the I.T.A. could feed programmes to a network of stations from a centralized commercial Radio 1, leaving a small proportion of the day to local contractors. The B.B.C. has perhaps three years to stop this, and a good many difficulties to overcome. There is 'needle time', for instance: this means that, under an agreement with the Musicians' Union and the record companies, Radio 1 and 2 can only play some 50 hours of records a week between them. Their controller, Robin Scott, concedes that it would be economical, as well as in keeping with the nature of the service, to expand this for Radio 1. Negotiations are no doubt under way already.

Then there is the problem of reception. The B.B.C. claims to have improved transmission on 247; but it has still been receiving complaints from thwarted listeners. The still battling Radio Caroline was coming across much more strongly in the south-east last weekend.

The B.B.C. will also face the problem of non-competition. When Caroline disappears (as surely it must) the pressure on Radio 1 to keep abreast of popular taste will relax. The disc jockeys could become overestablished, the programmes static—and, in a few years, Radio 1 could seem as dated as the Light Programme does now. Then we would presumably have to endure the tedious hubbub of another 'revolution'.[1]

One of the more tangible results of the spread of this instantly available music has been a decline in record sales. One record company carried out a survey comparing record-buying in the Home Counties, where the pirate stations can be received, and in Cardiff, where they cannot. They found that record sales were up to 20 per cent higher in the latter. This is a reaction which cannot please Radio Luxembourg, at least 25 per cent of whose time is paid for directly by the record companies.

Radio Luxembourg—'The Station of the Stars'—was beaming commercials broadcasts at this country long before any of the pirate stations, though its mixture and approach resemble theirs. Luxembourg, however, only broadcast at night, and in the early hours of the morning dissolves into light

---

[1] Benedict Nightingale, 'The Phoney Revolution' in *New Society*, 5 October, 1967.

orchestral music. (Which perhaps explains why the station's audience is so evenly spread over different age groups, with 34 per cent between twenty-five and forty-four, and 30 per cent over forty-five.)

Luxembourg's disc jockeys have the same chummy ring-master's voices that boom from London and Caroline, though thankfully with a little less hysteria, and a little less gilt. But their comfortableness is actually institutionalized: Radio Luxembourg's Station Policy contains this stipulation, remark-able in a democracy, and certainly helpful in keeping pop estranged from the real world.

(The following are not permitted:) References, jokes or songs concerning any reigning Monarch, Members of Parliament, the Cabinet or any branch of Her Majesty's Government or any other government, politics or political figures, subjects that may be regarded as having an indirect political significance nationally or internationally, religion, other advertisers, physical deformi-ties, or any other reference, joke or song considered to be in questionable taste.

Even I.T.V.'s charter is not as strict as this. But then I.T.V., unlike Luxembourg (and American commercial broadcasting), does not run shows which are directly sponsored by advertisers. On Luxembourg, roughly thirteen hours' listening time a week is bought by record companies, and given over exclusively to their own records. E.M.I. give each of their new releases a 'plug rating', which is an indication of the number of plays it is to be given during the company's broadcasting time. A plug rating of one, which would be given to a record by a well-established group, or a new one that showed great promise, indicates that there are to be seven plays a week. A rating of two brings four plays, and a rating of three, two. On the B.B.C. there can be no such organized plugging. The most that the publicity men can do is to suggest to a disc jockey or pro-gramme producer that a particular record is worth playing. There are plenty of free luncheons and gifts, but probably no direct financial bribes. Peter Leslie, who handled publicity for Lonnie Donegan and Acker Bilk, has stated that 'there is as a matter of simple fact no payola whatsoever on this side of the Atlantic'.[1] Certainly D.J.'s as successful as Pete Murray and David Jacobs (the latter is estimated to be earning about £30,000 a year) can afford to play, within reason, exactly what they like.

The effects of any sort of plugging are complex and unpredictable. The more frequently a record is played, the sooner familiarity and affection build up amongst the listeners. But beyond a certain stage the audience may feel that there is no point in buying a record that they can hear ten times a day on the radio. And beyond a slightly further stage, boredom, and even annoyance, may set in. The evidence is that, although plugging can help to make a single record successful, it can never establish an artist or a craze. Lennon and MacCartney's *Michelle* was pushed to saturation on most radio stations, and by the end of January 1966 had reached the Number One spot, and had over forty cover versions made of it. But records like Lonnie Donegan's *Rock Island Line*, and the Beatles' first, *Love Me Do* (both of which marked the beginning of radical new trends), were only plugged after the record companies had realized that they were *already* immensely popular with teenagers.

The prima donnas

If the communicators help to shape the pop scene by refusing to criticize it, the men behind the artists condition it by refusing to leave it alone. All the major singers and groups have a host of assistants to produce and market their music. There are Artists and Repertoire men (A. & R.), usually attached to record companies, to choose and record the songs they put on disc; road managers to organize their transport and take care of their equipment; publicity men to handle their advertising; and to control the whole circus—the manager himself. Some remarkable men have occupied this position. Colonel Tom Parker for Elvis Presley, Brian Epstein for the Beatles. Epstein once described the manager's role in this way:

[1] *Fab: the Anatomy of a Phenomenon*, MacGibbon & Kee, 1965.

What I've done, and what I'm doing, is to spot people who would record discs that *I* think from my experience of selling records would sell in a big way. But you need something more than is required to make—or sell—*one* recording. You need somebody who you can rely on to go on and make *several* good records.

More than that, you need people who have the personal qualities and colourful character to stand up to—and exploit—the various forms of publicity that are necessary to keep their records before the public. You have to be a judge of what kinds of people teenagers want to hear singing attractive music, and out of those you need to be able to select the ones who are capable of having a kind of continuous folklore built up about them, so that the public wants to go on hearing *about* them, as well as hearing *from* them.[1]

The building of this 'continuous folklore' around the idols necessarily involves changing the pattern of their lives. Sometimes this means no more than a slight alteration in their dress. Epstein advised the Beatles to drop the leather jackets and jeans, which they had worn whilst playing in Hamburg and Liverpool, though he allowed them to choose their own substitutes. The fancy waistcoats and bowler hats that were Acker Bilk's trademark were the result of some complicated historical and psychological reasoning by his publicity man, Peter Leslie.

Occasionally more drastic physical changes are imposed on the artist. He may, for instance, he put on a slimming diet, have his nose reshaped and his teeth straightened, be given contact lenses, built-up shoes and a new hair colour. His own name or that of his group may be repeatedly changed to fit the tone of the current fashion. Unfortunately, one month's style may be the next month's anachronism. One of the more pathetic sights of the pop scene is the repeated 'débuts' of the same vaguely familiar sets of faces, as, with new uniforms and labels, they struggle to dissociate themselves from their previous outworn image.

There is no doubt that many of the lesser known groups are grossly maltreated by their agents and managers in this way.

[1] The *Observer*, 17 May, 1964.

But there is very little that they can do about it; being novices, they have nothing to bargain with. To gain entry into the recording world at all they may have to sign lopsided long-term contracts that give the businessmen complete control over their image and recorded material for up to three years. The entrepreneurs, for their part, know that one new group pushed quickly to the top, with all the side-money this will earn from T.V. shows and royalties, is worth a dozen established singers who never quite make the Top Fifty. So they will package a vulnerable new group for instant success, disregarding the fact that by so doing they are almost certainly prejudicing their long-term progress. But then almost everyone benefits from the rise of a new group or craze, from the D.J.'s to the record salesgirls. Only the currently popular small-time groups suffer, as their music is discarded into pop's lumberroom. To survive they must adjust, or change their jobs. So, like long-suffering chameleons, they adapt—or, more probably, are adapted—and the whole vicious cycle starts again.

Much of the 'continuous folklore' is, like this, a simple result of the arduous process of living as a pop star. Within six months of playing in the village hall a successful seventeen-year-old singer can be travelling round the world. The Beatles, when their average age was less than twenty-three, played at the Shea Stadium, New York, before 55,600 people, which at that time was the largest audience ever recorded for an entertainer in the world. At the very least, the young singer will have to keep to a tight schedule of exhausting overnight coach trips, press conferences and recording dates. He will miss meals and rarely get to bed before the early hours of the morning. To keep in touch with his fans he will play seasons of one-night stands, visiting on consecutive nights places as far apart as Glasgow and Bristol. And wherever he goes *Rave* and *Jackie* and *Fabulous* will follow him, convinced by their readership figures that teenagers want to know more about their idols than they learn from a brief stage appearance:

Cliff Richard plans to get away from it all to a secret, sunsoaked hideaway. So do some of his famous friends—like Frank Ifield and Bruce Welch. In *Rave*, Britain's brightest and biggest colour monthly, the location is revealed. You can read, too, of the places the Rolling Stones choose to spend their spare time . . . Brenda Lee tells the poignant story behind her baby's struggle for survival . . . When a Beatle said 'Marry me' to the girl he loved, neither of them knew of the tragedy that lay ahead. How could they have foreseen that their life together was not to be? The full story of a Beatle's courtship is told by the girl he planned to marry—in *Rave*, out now, the sparkling colour monthly that pop fans can't afford to be without.[1]

The more enthusiastic fans are not satisfied by these vicarious insights, and follow their idols around in person. Some seem to be able to discover their most closely guarded movements. Others throw up their jobs to take temporary employment in towns where there is a summer pop season. One of Cliff Richard's fans was almost superhumanly persistent:

> This one, every Saturday night she is out front, then at the end of the show she is out the back waiting. She follows us to Bradford, Manchester, everywhere, stays the night at the same hotel, just for a glimpse. She's even booked a room facing the lift so that he couldn't possibly get in without her seeing him, but of course the next morning, when we drive off in a coach, she is left behind. So she gets a taxi, gives the driver a couple of quid and tells him to follow us as far as the two quid then stop and put her out. She's waving at us the whole time from the taxi. And somehow she always catches up with us.[2]

Some fans are less timorous: Billy J. Kramer was badly mauled on stage in Australia when hysterical girls broke through the police cordons. It is common for coins, sweets and toys to be thrown at singers during a performance, ironically as a mark of approval. The evasive tactics which the performers employ are equally theatrical. The Beatles went unscathed into one theatre by disguising themselves in borrowed policemen's helmets. And the following safety manœuvres undertaken during one of their visits to America, are now almost routine:

[1] Advertisements for *Rave*.
[2] Cliff Richard's road manager, Bob Ferrier, in *The Wonderful World of Cliff Richard*, Peter Davies, 1964.

To get them to the coach was itself a major security operation. They were smuggled down a service lift in their Atlantic City hotel and into a laundry van which took them to a limousine more than a mile away. The limousine took them to a bus parked in a quiet cul-de-sac on the city's outskirts.

A police escort for the bus would have drawn other motorists' attention to it. Instead, a helicopter hovered over the road half a mile ahead maintaining radio contact with police cars and motor cycles standing by if required.

The operation was a success. The seemingly empty coach made its way to the back of the Philadelphia Convention Hall without attracting the slightest attention from tens of thousands of waiting fans, who could have flattened it as easily as they crushed the limousine waiting to take the Beatles away from their earlier show in Seattle.[1]

The story is told that the Canadian singer Paul Anka, when he was performing in Atlantic City, used to look at people in the streets through a telescope. 'This is the nearest I can get,' he said, 'without the cops watching me.'

All this takes its inevitable toll. The young pop star acquires, before his time, a free-wheeling sophistication and a certain world-weariness. Perhaps this is part of his appeal. But slimmed, photographed, disguised as a policeman, shunted down service lifts, and cut off for simple reasons of survival from ordinary communications with the public, he also becomes a commodity: at best, a mere performer. The high-tension life that the pop singer is forced to lead is, alongside the indiscriminate enthusiasms of the D.J.s, another constraint on the quality of his music. The ruthless suddenness with which the less-than-vigilant artist can vanish from the scene compels him to be for ever in the public eye, for ever producing new records before he has got new ideas. He has little time to relax and think, little chance to travel unnoticed, meet new friends and broaden his experience in a way that might enrich his songs.

[1] From a report in the *New Musical Express*, 27 March, 1964.

Nor dare he bite the hand that signs his contracts and sing what he really thinks of this rootless life of tawdry hotels and one-night women. So until his conscience, his nerves or the next idol in line get the better of him, he does his job.

There are few singers who have remained inside the pop idiom and matured consistently as artists. Some, like Alan Price and Brian Auger, have advanced by sacrificing a mass audience and exploring the fringelands between jazz and beat music. Many, like the Animals and the Rolling Stones, have become master craftsmen in the vein in which they started. But as yet very few have achieved the sort of steady maturation of style that we have come to expect from, say, average-good actors and novelists. Saddest of all, there are artists like Bob Dylan (whose case is considered in more detail in the next chapter) whose luminous talents have been seriously endangered since they entered the madcap rush for the Hit Parade.

A commonly chosen alternative to artistry in the pop world is the role of the prima donna, and the manufacture of individuality by the easy tricks of sensationalism and exhibitionism:

> I'll tell you a funny thing that happened that time. During my act I get wild, you know. I kind of let myself go. Anyway, I split one of my patent leather shoes, and I was going to throw it in the dustbin. Then I thought: 'I know what I'll do. I'll wear it when I do the next performance—the split doesn't show that much—and I'll fling it into the audience. Some girl would be thrilled and that's better than putting it in the bin.' I ended up in bare feet on the stage. And I saw the girl who got the shoe actually biting it. Great.[1]

Heinz, and all those other performers who throw their metaphorical shoes to the fans, belong more with the operators than with their fellow singers. Their prime interest is not in whipping up their music but in whipping up their audience. Many other pop stars excite their audiences, but these evangelists are peculiar in doing it quite deliberately, as the main aim of their performance. P. J. Proby, the most notorious protagonist of these techniques, explained in a radio interview with

[1] *New Musical Express*, 28 February, 1964.

the psychologist, William Sargant, how he uses many of the tricks of the Southern Baptist preacher.[1] His tremulous, exaggerated voice, and his songs carefully arranged in order of mounting excitement, can work up a frenzy (in the front rows of the audience at least) that can reach close to conversion-pitch. Luckily, P.J. has nothing to sell except himself. But' many of the tricks he uses would make even the most opportunist bible-puncher blush. During the early part of 1965 he used to split his trousers quite regularly during stage appearances, to reveal an expanse of white, velvet underpants.

A performer who used more macabre techniques was Screaming Lord Sutch. He began many of his stage shows by rising sepulchrally from an upstage coffin, his eighteen-inch-long hair gushing from beneath a top hat. Sutch explained his technique this way:

> It's some kind of weird kick . . . you can get lost in it. Get some sort of message over to the audience, some sort of tension in the air.
>
> Some of the kids think I'm an absolute madman. They say: 'He's horrible, when's he coming back?' Face it, good artists don't get on . . . Sometimes T.V. companies say to me, if you get your hair cut and wear a wig, we'll put you on. Face it, it's the class system. I got lots more acts. In one I'm announced as King Kong and I come on in a cage on wheels. I wait till a couple of little girls in the front row throw sweet-papers, then I collapse the cage and pounce out.[2]

The last time I saw Lord Sutch perform, just after he had notched up a few score votes in the 1964 General Election, there was no tension in the air. Just ridicule.

For less melodramatic performers girls still rush the stage, wet their seats and sob. But it's doubtful whether they suffer much psychological damage as a result: there are worse ways of releasing tension, and more infamous figures they could choose as agents of their catharsis. The common perplexity of adults at the sight of teenagers drowning the very music they have apparently come to hear also misses the point. In fact, the

[1] *Third Programme*, 28 December, 1965.
[2] *New Statesman*, 16 August, 1963.

audience have not come for the music, which they already know by heart from records. (In any case, the acoustics in most cinemas and dance halls is usually bad enough to rule out any acceptable rendering.) What they are interested in is the singer's *presence*, his power of invoking and dramatizing the sustaining myths of contemporary adolescence. Peter Laurie found a neat analogy in *Teenage Revolution*:

> . . . the atmosphere is more like a corrida, where the performer is pitted against the audience, where with a guitar for a cape he has to show his mettle. The teenagers look, very simply for vitality, for identity with themselves. The pop singer is an assertion that they too are vital, attractive. His music and performance are simply vehicles for demonstrating these qualities. In a way this is a narcissistic stage in the development of the teenage society; in which it looks at itself in the hope that its members can overtop the adults in the mystique of entertainment and communications. It is noticeable, too, how the acts are very simple and unprofessional by grown-up standards: this is important, because to be professional, particularly in entertainment, means an adherence to the established corpus of rules concerning the behaviour of entertainers, and these are made and maintained by adults. There is no way in which the young can be professional without belonging to the disliked and square adult world because so far there is no set standard for teenager performers.[1]

That the scream syndrome is a conventional, ritualistic response, rather than a spontaneous overflow of dangerously uncontrollable emotion, is well illustrated (in different ways) by these two comments. The first is from Brian Epstein:

> I saw a girl sitting in the front row the other night. She had her hands to her head and she was screaming—you know 'Aieee'—you say screaming, but they're not shouting 'Help!' or 'Murder!'. In the middle of it, her handbag dropped off her lap. She stopped screaming, bent down, picked it up, had a quick inspection to make sure nothing had fallen out or got broken, put it back safely between her thigh and the edge of the seat so it wouldn't fall again, put her hands to her head, and started up again 'Aieeeee!'. That's not hysteria. That's self-expression.[2]

[1] *Teenage Revolution*, Anthony Blond, 1965.
[2] *The Observer*, 17 May, 1964.

(So P. J. Proby gets pawed by teenagers on *Ready, Steady, Go!* where it's usual, and politely left alone on *Top of the Pops*, where it's not; the Rolling Stones are ignored by girls in the blasé surroundings of Carnaby Street, yet are mobbed by the same girls in a cinema a couple of miles away.) The second comment is from a letter in *Disc*:

> Why do people keep telling us to stop pulling the Walker Brothers off stage? Don't they know we can't help it?
> With the help of others, I have managed to pull Scott off stage, so I know. Honest, when he held his hands out we just couldn't help ourselves. He didn't get hurt. He fell on top of us.[1]

Discs: The ritual for the home: December, 1966

My old man—move over, Nigel Barton—my old man built himself a real radio about 1925. My mind's eye still retains the view through the playpen bars of its sloping black front with dials, and mad-scientist-type thermionic valves sticking out the top. It was the first of a series extending almost to the beginning of the War, and on them he listened to the Wednesday symphony concerts two weeks out of every three (he was on the wrong shift the third week), to the organ recitals and the chamber concerts and *The Foundations of Music*, week in and week out. The point is less that, as a result, Beethoven is just Muzak to me, but that for him steam radio was/is a real university of the air long before that nice Mr Wilson coined the phrase. He must have been Lord Reith's perfect listener.

And both he and his lordship, as we now know, were wrong. The destiny of a medium that can do that to Beethoven was to fill the silent places with low-protein tinkle-tinkle, cover the cracks in the conversation with auricular wallpaper. However H.M. Government make their peace with pop-around-the-clock, it will be belated recognition of this fact, after over 40 years of trying to force radio to do the other thing.

There wasn't much excuse for getting it wrong, for this was not the first technocultural revolution that betrayed the hopes of its intellectual proponents. Never mind what happened to universal literacy, the gramophone disaster was in full flop at the very time that the B.B.C. was being chartered. By the twenties the

[1] *Disc Weekly*, 22 January, 1966.

full extent to which Edison's phonograph had been misconstrued should have been plain to see.

The misconstruction began with the name bestowed on the basic unit of gramoculture. As is clear from our continued use of the word record, we persist in the simple-minded supposition that the function of the gramophone is to store great sounds for posterity (like The Congressional Record). Yet the moment the gramophone became an industry its social function became less preservative than distributive, to make any and every sound immediately available at any point on the earth's surface to which a portable gramophone could go.

As a distributive device, of course, it has been overrun by radio, which provides instant sound without fussing over vinyl discs. So the gramophone gets pushed up the first step of the retreat into specialization to which all technically outmoded media (films, for instance, not to mention books) must submit. The gramophone becomes a system for distributing deviant sound to disaffected cultural minorities whose peculiar tastes are not satisfied by the continuous wallpaper provided by radio—I mean, if you were interested in good music would you listen to the Music Programme? And don't forget that the audience for pop is not a mass, quote-unquote, but a seethe of warring and incompatible minorities. One thing the trade never tells you is how few discs you need sell to get into the Top Twenty in a thin week.

So, for someone like myself, for whom the auricular wallpaper service never provides enough Stockhausen (but too much Boulez), never enough of les Surfs (but always too much of dreary Pet Clark), nothing like enough Ian and Sylvia (but more than enough Julie Felix), the gramophone is the natural resource to satisfy these kinky tastes. Repeat kinky; down here in the vinyl deeps (as Tom Wolfe calls them) we are all deviants from the going standards of society at large.

Gramoculture, in an apparently middle position—like the movies—between live performance and an all-pervasive electronic surrogate, is unlike the movies in being far kinkier. When you stop and think, its rituals are extraordinarily odd; retiring to glass-fronted, numbered, sound-proofed cubicles looks, in cold blood, more like Hirshfeld's Sexual Anomalies than 363 Oxford Street.

Not that there is any real acoustic privacy when you get inside there. What's the use of having a delicate trickle of Charles Spinks piped through to booth number what's-it when the whole building is writhing with those Good Vibrations? The booth bit is pure ritual, as witness those elbow-length mini-booths hung on the walls of the pop shops. In spite of all that simulated acoustic tiling on the inside, they aren't soundproof worth a damn. The only reason you can hear your selected disc is that the loudspeaker is practically down your earhole.

But these peculiar rituals of purchase (what you select from the rack is not the disc at all, but its empty sleeve, in most cases) simply mirror the very odd psychology of record ownership. The coming festive season will produce a proliferation of cases of the following characteristic syndrome: cool, trendy householders will go into record shops to buy some any-old-thing type LPs to make wallpaper for a party, sweat blood all afternoon over the choice and come out with Andre Benichou's Guitar Bach, for instance, or a good bouzouki album, hide it before the party begins, and play it continuously for the following week.

For some reason, or reasons, you can't treat a flat vinyl disc with spiral grooves on both sides as wallpaper. In the absence of some straight market research on the topic, one can only hazard guesses at these reasons. One could be that those vinyl discs have people in them. After four centuries of academic portrait painting had made an unattainable ideal of 'the speaking likeness', Edison invented a mechanical process that couldn't produce anything else.

Furthermore, it only speaks when you make it. There must be a power of atavism behind the sense of personal possession that comes from the fact of command—to be able to summon up vast symphonies in the privacy of your own home, or, more subtly and sadistically, to force Fischer-Dieskau to go back and sing that again, and again.

The fact that you can have Sandie Shaw on the hearthrug right between the stereo speakers, any night, on demand, makes the gramophone one step towards that standard science-fiction heaven/hell of being able to dial up synthetic pleasure-people. But that step will be another retreat into perverse specialisation as soon as the next link-up should come along—and telly is beginning to show us one already. Notoriously, there are a number of pop groups that 'wouldn't exist without television', and the whole point of *I'm a Boy* is that the words were seen to be issuing from the faces of the Who, than which nothing could be more unpleasantly male. Already it becomes difficult to listen to Sonny and Cher if one can't see Cher—all right, I'm a fan, but that's the point.

Take the Stones, for instance. Great Bafflement that they have difficulty in getting a disc up to Number One, yet their concerts are still Standing Room Only and the fans are screaming louder than ever. The sound on its own doesn't mean a thing, I suspect, if you can't actually see Mick Jagger deliberately provoking the dollies to climb right over the policemen and maul him. Come the first cheap domestic video-tape machine that can give you that in the girl's dorm, and it will be bye-bye vinyl discs.

Meanwhile, back at real life, there is something else that kinks gramoculture: its air of being uncensored, outside social control. The odd Welsh cleric may try to call down hellfire on Jock Strapp LPs, and Auntie BBC may occasionally try to pretend a pop record doesn't exist, but how long did the famous anti-Beatles campaign last? No analogy with the moving-body arts applies here—movies and telly have inherited their own versions of the codes that society had evolved for the stage, but society has never come to terms with packaged sounds.

So, the shops around Times Square and 42nd Street cheerfully display LPs (*He's the Queen of Fire Island*) that aren't half as blue as they pretend to be, but are vastly more blue than any stag movie that could be so publicly sold, more suggestive than any paperback in the adjoining rack. And if you don't consider this any great credit to the age of McLuhan, the flip side of the coin is that some of the most durable monuments to current movements for the liberation of the person and the personality are the uncensorable L.P.s of Joan Baez.

'Durable monuments' yet? The gramophone does preserve, but it preserves best its vinyl children. Pondering this problem, I put Dionne Warwick's old original L.P. on for the first time in about 18 months, and it is—to coin a phrase—riveting. I had forgotten how good she was, how brilliant the backings, and how some A. & R. genius had ordered the tracks into a song cycle as conclusive and satisfying as *Frauenlieben Und Leben*. Better, even, because it deals with some even more intensely female emotions.

And, though other birds will sing Lieder and other sopranos will sing Burt Bacharach, this particular performance as it exists on the disc (and probably never existed in 'real life') is unrepeatable. What the record preserves is not something that was going to be said or sung anyhow—Great Performances on Record are

E

usually a great bore, even as archaeology—but things that were specifically addressed to the microphone for recording, and have thereby acquired a quality that is not present in performances to which recording is incidental. I know that—as a talking performer—I speak differently to a microphone in a studio from the way I address a microphone that some tape addict has thrust between me and a live audience.

The studio microphone, though inanimate, is intimate, and the weird chemistry of the special vinyl relationship starts at that same point. Even at a big session, when the microphones hang around the studio almost as numerous as the instrumentalists, each performer tends to address himself to his own, local microphone—indeed, he had better, or the balance will be shot to hell—and there, again, the secret, uncensored affair between recorded performer and the recording-hearer begins. Just as hi-fi-trained operatic audiences now expect of theatres acoustic performances which no building could ever hope to offer, so an increasing audience expects of the live performer the special intimacies that only the recording can give.

Don't complain that singers nowadays can't make themselves heard without a mike. Often they could, but that's not the point. Down among the vinyl deviates the microphone is the necessary and reassuring symbol of a relationship that is as special as that indicated by a masonic grip or a rose behind the right ear.[1]

The operators are not able to guarantee success to any artist or craze. *Ready, Steady, Go!* can popularise a dance—if the mods are already doing it—and plugs on the pirate stations can help isolated records into the Hit Parade. But beyond this the development of fashion is very largely up to the moods and whims of the teenage audience. They pay their six-and-eightpences and they take their choice; and the choice is not always the one that the impresarios would like.

But on the *quality* of pop music the operators' influence is much greater. The lunatic energy which a performer needs to survive in the pop scene (and which is as much a result of managerial pushing as of the inherent demands of the scene) is a very real check on any talent he may possess. And, in a

[1] Reyner Banham, 'Vinyl Deviationa' in *New Society*, 1 December, 1966.

popular mass music, quality is to some extent dependent upon audience response, and this is a factor which is highly susceptible to conditioning. The deliberate manipulation of teenage audiences by some singers helps create a pattern of response that makes *what* they sing irrelevant. And it's not difficult to be lulled into listening to Dodd and Dylan in the same way when the disc jockeys encapsulate both of them in the same desensitizing chatter.

Perhaps the operators' biggest crime is just this: that by their refusal to discriminate, their reluctance to criticise, they have helped create a shock-absorber between a cosy, comfortable pop scene and a rather different world. There is a widespread aversion to the idea that pop could be thoughtful as well as being fun, and to the possibility that everybody (in the audience at least) would benefit from critical public discussions of pop music. Just how far this is an authentic attitude of the teenage audience may become a little clearer in the next chapter.

6   Protest music: a case history*

We have talked so far about the general processes by which new fashions are generated in the teenage audience, and about the ways in which some of the practices of the operators condition the content and effect of these fashions. To separate the influence of these two institutions in the development of any one particular fashion is much more difficult. ('Workers' control' in the pop industry, for instance, is increasingly closing the gap between audience and operators.)

But, providentially, there occurred in the summer of 1965 a small but critical craze in which were crystallized many of the arguments we have been touching upon. 'Protest' music was not a very long-lived fad, nor in statistical terms a very successful one. But it aroused a spirited controversy and left a faint but seemingly permanent impression on our popular music. It had, in theory, every element that a truly popular form should have, and suffered, in practice, every injury that can befall such a form as it is shunted through our mass communications networks.

It was, to start with, a response to 'lived contemporary experience': to Lyndon Johnson's napalm bombs, and the Alabama cops' cattle-probes. It developed exclusively amongst the teenage audience, in rhythm and blues clubs in Richmond, and campus revolts in California, where a new generation of students were starting to question the greatness of the Great Society. It wedded together the folk tradition of social comment with the tough electronic beat of an urban dance-hall rock.

[1] February, 1966.

In fact, it was difficult to imagine how a music could have been more relevant and contemporary.

When some of these songs began making seditious inroads into the Hit Parade, it was difficult not to feel delighted that they were reaching such a large public. But then—and in retrospect it seems to have been inevitable—things started to go wrong. An unofficial consensus amongst disc jockeys and pop journalists brought about the pinpointing, clustering together and labelling of these songs as 'protest music'. A new craze had been filed. Immediately, while the phrase still sounded big and angry, singers who had not had a hit record for some time began producing songs that were as trite and generalized in their comments on war and freedom as most pop songs are on love. Because of the lack of discrimination in the pop scene, these camp followers put everybody's sincerity in question, and protest music, as a fashion, died a quick and rather embarrassing death. (Though those singers who had originated it went back to performing before their small but steadily growing audiences.) In one singer, Bob Dylan, a version of this cycle was enacted in cameo form. Dylan began as a conventional folk-singer, matured into our first truly contemporary song-writer and lapsed finally into passing off as songs an increasing volume of unfinished, introspective lyric fragments. In three years Dylan showed just how good pop music could be, and just how easy it was for a singer involved with a mass audience to abort his material.

Not in front of the children

Not many people inside the modern pop music business have ever been bothered about pop's lack of contact with our contemporary concerns. Most of the nagging about this has come from the outside, and has consequently been ignored. To entertain is now not just one of pop music's ambitions—it is the limit of its aims. Pressurized by sheer custom and the danger of disturbing a comfortable and receptive audience, the songwriters have stuck to safe, impersonal subjects. (This is a strangely anomalous convention, for the same young people who—however accidentally—have avoided overt sex, crime and war in their songs, will flock to the cinemas and bookstalls for proxy excursions into these areas.) And so strong is the allied belief that the appeal of lyrics is insignificant by the side of that of the sound and artist, that frequently singers don't bother to make their words decipherable, and listeners don't try to decipher them. Many of the Rolling Stones best lyrics have been so much background noise because of this.

In spite of the superficial shaking it was given by the protest craze, this overall indifference to lyrics has remained standard practice in the pop world. The only other serious challenge it has received has been from the crash songs. Since *Tell Laura I Love Her*, there have been perhaps half a dozen numbers which have related the death of some boy in a motor-cycle pile-up, and the subsequent despair of his intended. Motor-cycle crashes are a sufficiently routine feature of teenage life, God knows, for this to be a thoroughly legitimate theme for a popular song. But unfortunately the level at which this *genre* operate is all too often that of the following song (*Terry* by Twinkle):

> He said that he wanted to be close by my side.
> We had a quarrel, I was untrue on the night he died,
> And it's too late to tell this boy how great he was.
> Please wait at the gates of Heaven for me, Terry.
> He rode into the night,
> Accelerated his motor-bike,
> I cried to him in fright,
> Don't do it, don't do it, don't do it.[1]

[1] This song brought forth a priceless letter in the *New Musical Express* of January 15, 1965:

How many more songs are going to be made about ton-up boys getting killed? With songs like *Terry* and *Leader of the Pack*, what is the pop world coming to? I don't mean to be nasty, but mods seem to take a delight in pulling Rockers to pieces. How do you think their parents feel when they hear songs like these, just after their son or daughter has gone out on their bikes? I can assure you that the boys themselves do not like these songs. . . . And if a Rocker made a song about a mod getting killed, it would get

The reactions of parents and authorities to these songs are invariably ones of shock and disgust. Letters about 'the glamourization of death' appear in the papers; radio stations inter the records in their archives. *Terry* was banned by I.T.V., in spite of Twinkle's protestations that it was a 'road-safety song'. The operators ran true to form. Nobody, to my knowledge, condemned the record because it was false and sentimental, but simply because it was about a 'distasteful' topic. Once again quality was immaterial (though I suspect that, if the song *had* been a tougher, more honest one, the bans would have been doubly ruthless).

Purists and puritans

But, in this country at least, the real precursors of the protest singers were away on the fringelands of pop, in the folk-music clubs of Birmingham, Newcastle and Liverpool. Here at least young people had the opportunity to sing honestly about politics and war, love and death, unmolested by the prudishness of the mass media. Politically, they were mostly left-wing, and musically some way from the English Folk Dance and Song Society. But sadly, many of their songs were little closer to the lives of modern 'folk' than the ballads popular in Cecil Sharp House.

British folk music has been through two major shake-ups since the days when the term meant little more to most people that the Hearts of Oak songs they were made to chant at school. The first was the skiffle craze, which brought to light a vast amount of early American folk-music. This was the first time that gospel music, cowboy ballads and work-songs had been widely heard in this country without the mellowing accompaniment of a dance orchestra or a music teacher's piano. Their impact was sufficiently strong to encourage many young people to continue singing and listening to folk-music after skiffle had faded.

nowhere. But when it's the other way around, it goes straight to the top. It's not only morbid—it's unfair.

Elvis Fan, Hucknall, Notts.

The other jolt was the Campaign for Nuclear Disarmament. Since people rarely bother to write serious songs when they're content, most good folk-song has been born out of social and political unrest. And there has rarely been an issue, the Spanish Civil War not-with-standing, which aroused such political unrest amongst the younger generation as the nuclear question. The majority of those hundreds of thousands who marched between Aldermaston and London during the early sixties were under the age of 25, and they carried their guitars with them. On another march at another time they might have kept themselves going with old favourites like *The Red Flag* and *Green Grow the Rushes, Oh.* But the sheer seriousness of the protest they were making seemed to demand something better than this. So new songs were written about peace and international understanding, that became amongst the first examples of folk-music to come out of our own times. Most of the songs, like *The H-Bombs Thunder*, were marching songs, and were bold, emotional and deliberately naïve:

> *Tell the leaders of the nations,*
> *Make the whole wide world take heed:*
> *Poison from the radiation*
> *Strikes at every race and creed.*
> *Must you put mankind in danger,*
> *Murder folk in distant lands?*
> *Will you bring death to a stranger,*
> *Have his blood upon your hands?*

(Significantly, the music for this song was not original, but a traditional tune called *Miners' Lifeguard.*)

Stimulated musically by skiffle and politically by C.N.D., the folk movement began to grow. There is now a smattering of programmes on radio and T.V. given over exclusively to folk, and clubs to cater for the music are springing up all over the country.

There are today three main types of folk-singer, if one omits for the moment artists like Joan Baez and Peter Seeger, who will sing everything from a good pop song to an unaccompanied ethnic ballad. They are so different in style and intention that it is monstrous to include them all together in the same category. But pop journalists have succeeded in doing this without any apparent discomfort, and it might be instructive to examine why.

The first group are more folksy than folk: singers like Marianne Faithfull and The Seekers. Their products are not strictly folk-songs at all—if this term means honest songs about contemporary life—but pop songs with a folk sound. Many of these are pleasant enough, but the mere addition of an acoustic guitar and some competent harmony singing does not transform a jingle into a sensitive personal statement. Complaints about the incorrect categorization of pop music are perhaps more irrelevant than the categorization itself: Dylan's *Like a Rolling Stone* is a good song, whether it's labelled (as it variously has been) folk, folk-rock, pop, protest or blues. But the indiscriminate use of the label 'folk' has been actually harmful. The grouping together of songs like the Seekers' *I'll Never Find Another You* and Donovan's *Universal Soldier* must encourage the assumption that Donovan was attempting to do no more with his gentle attack on military obedience that the Seekers were with their melodious magazine story.

At the opposite extreme to these performers are the purists, who have been fighting what amounts to a holy war against the 'commercialization' of folk music. The purists' attitudes are very clear. They believe that the essence of folk-song lies in the oral tradition, in the circulation, in small, intimate groups, of musical and lyrical comments on the lives of ordinary people. They are insistent that this sort of intensely stylized music, which relies so much on subtle voice timbres, regional dialects and fluid vocal interpretations, cannot retain its vitality and honesty if it moves out of the face-to-face situation into the mass media. Some would even go further and say that it loses most of its special qualities if the voice is de-emphasized by an accompanying instrument.

Understandably enough the purists main interest has been in the unearthing and keeping alive of our country's traditional music. But some, like Johnny Handle, have tried to orchestrate contemporary situations in the dialect and speech rhythms of traditional ballads.

> *When the coal's fired doon the shu'ls de fly and the belts get*
> *   loaded full,*
> *'Til, in half as hoor, a lump gans by and the motor will not*
> *   pull.*
> *Brocken belt; is the cry an' we aall craall oot te the mother-*
> *   gate, it te mend.*
> *Geordie Hall, he's the deppity in wor flat, says:*
> *   Ye'll drive us roond the bend.*
> *Oh, the collier lad is a canny lad an' he's allways of gud cheer,*
> *An' he knaa's how te work,*
> *An' he knaa's how te shork,*
> *An' he knaa's how te sup gud beor.   (The Filler)*

But for all the invaluable work which they have done in preserv-
ing a dying tradition, the purists have done a disservice to
popular music as a whole by their repeated dogmatic attacks
on all styles other than their own. The following passage, by
Tristram P. Coffin, editor of the Journal of American Folklore,
is typical:

> Popular folk music is music tailored to a pre-conditioned mass
> taste, and like popular jazz, popular blues, popular calypso and
> popular hill music is a conventional, monotonous, trite package
> that conventional, monotonous, trite minds (left-wing, suburban,
> rural . . . as the case may be) will buy in the supermarkets of
> the entertainment industry. To me, Bob Dylan, Frank Sinatra
> and Hank Snow are one and the same . . . their distinctions super-
> ficial, created only by the immediate vogue they capitalised upon.[1]

It must be said that many of the purists' songs are themselves
trite and monotonous, and the lyrics often as sentimental as
any Donald Peers weepie. I once watched a Geordie folk-singer
produce from his coat pocket a minute concertina that he had
'found in the hold of an uncle's fishing boat' and proceed to
play on it a quite tuneless dirge that lasted twelve minutes.
Certainly nothing justifies the purist's contention that their
music is the only real folk-music and therefore the only real

[1] 'Folk Songs and the Top 40' in *Sing Out*, February–March 1966.

popular music. As Big Bill Broonzy once remarked 'I guess all songs is folk songs; I never heard no horse sing 'em'.

Even in the context of areas like Tyneside, pseudo-traditional ballads, judged as *folk* songs, would seem to be dangerously nostalgic. One would not know from them that there is massive redevelopment proposed for Newcastle, a New Town rising at Washington, and that bowling alleys are becoming as popular as the working men's clubs. Most of the ballads are as romantic and impersonal in their expression of the quality of northern life as conventional pop songs are of teenage love. The collier lad may be a canny lad but he still has a good chance of being buried alive or contracting phthisis. And if he lives in Jarrow he has an even better chance of being amongst the persistent 6 per cent unemployed.

The value of traditional ballads to contemporary music lies not so much in the possibility of forcing modern content into their old idioms, but in the way their proved and effective formal techniques are *reworked* to meet new situations:

> There is a certain analogy with a masked ball, where by assuming a formal mask, you shed the one that you wear the rest of the time. The very element of tradition, to which anyone who gets involved in folk-song to any real extent is going to get exposed, can nourish a kind of individualism which can then go on to grow, to integrate, to propagate—and to remove the mask . . . But so far as the refugee aspect is concerned, what is most important about excursions into the culture of other times or places is what you bring back, and what you do with it. Otherwise it's just escapism, and essentially sterile. It's possible to take folk-song in this way, and much good may it do you; sing sea shanties in order to feel tough and identify with the men who made them. . . . Whereas the *purpose* of a shanty is to help you keep on working...[1]

The last group of folk-singers, the puritans, are really a sub-division of the purists, with whom they share a deep distrust of commercial popular music. They differ mainly in their concern

[1] Kevin McGrath, 'What have they done to the folk'? in *Anarchy*, May 1965. The writer of this article underlined his points by composing a song called *I've Got a Secret* to the tune of *I Love a Lassie* during a C.N.D. demonstration at the Reading Regional Seat of Government!

to try and extend, tentatively, the idioms of traditional music to embrace modern themes. So whilst maintaining many of the modal chord structures and vocal embellishments of anti-quarian folk music, singers like Ewan MacColl have incorporated into their vocabularies Appalachian banjo licks and lyrics about motorways and railways:

> *When you've done your time at the loco-shed and had your*
> *   share of trouble,*
> *On the old footplate, you're the driver's mate,*
> *And you're married to a lousy shovel.*
> *It's check the water, check the tools and check the blooming*
> *   coal in,*
> *Give the gauge a wipe, check injector pipe, now it's*
> *Swing your shovel at the double, give her rock, watch the*
> *   clock,*
> *Steam raising, sweat running, back aching, bone shaking,*
> *Fireman! Fireman! keep her rolling.   (The Iron Road)*

I've called this group the puritans because all their songs exude this sense of grimy pride, this patronizing, non-con-formist veneration of the working classes and the dignity of manual labour. Given the background of the average folk-song writer such an attitude rarely produces convincing songs. In the above ballad, for instance, there is no communicated sense of any *personal* experience or understanding of railway work; nor can we believe that what Ewan MacColl is articulating on behalf of the engine drivers is what they feel about their jobs, either in fact or fantasy. He certainly hasn't created a proto-type for a contemporary music for the manual worker, who has little desire to relive his uncomfortable labours in song.

Like the Irish ganger I came across on a spur of the M2 in Kent. We talked, and then I asked one of those trite, reporter's ques-tions. He looked at me. 'Worksongs?' he said—and never had I been told more gently and in one word, from a man who plainly had the gift of words, that I had asked an idiotic question. 'No,' he said, 'we do not.'[1]

[1] Terry Coleman, 'The Elite Inside the Tunnel' in *New Society*, 6 January, 1966.

The middle-class intellectual, be he reporter or song-writer, has failed time and time again to understand the attitude of the modern manual worker towards his work. His misty, William Morris vision of the building site as the storehouse of lost or, if you're lucky, just un-self-consciously used skills is at total variance with the network of brute economic activity which it is in reality. Nor will the medicinal theory work: 'celebration' of bricklaying in song won't turn the jerry-builder into a master craftsman.

We can see a clue to the origins of this attitude if we look at the analogous phenomenon in the States. Charles Keil, in his masterly book *Urban Blues*, describes how the same 'moldy fig' mentality is manifest in many American intellectual's approach to the blues. To be 'true blue' in their opinion, the singer must satisfy the following criteria:

> Old age: the performer should preferably be more than sixty years old, blind, arthritic and toothless (as Lonnie Johnson put it when first approached for an interview, 'Are you another one of those guys who wants to put crutches under my ass?'). Obscurity: the blues singer should not have performed in public or have made a recording in at least twenty years; among deceased bluesmen, the best seem to be those who appeared in a big city one day in the 1920's, made from four to six recordings, and then disappeared into the countryside forever. Correct tutelage: the singer should have played with or been taught by some legendary figure. Agrarian milieu: a bluesman should have lived the bulk of his life as a sharecropper, coaxing mules and picking cotton, uncontaminated by city influences.[1]

The reason for this is not difficult to see. For the white liberal, the Noble Savage/lovable coon stereotype is an easier one to handle (and to feel sorry for) than the aggressive, cynical and perhaps even wealthy urban hustler. For Uncle Tom read John Bull and you have a precise translation to the British folk music scene.

Two examples, to conclude. First, *Go Down You Murderers*, a Ewan MacColl song about a subject as acid as the dubious hanging of Timothy Evans that is wrapped up nevertheless in a

[1] Charles Keil, *Urban Blues*, University of Chicago Press, 1966.

rollicking, beer-supping tune, and nineteenth-century sentence construction:

> *Tim Evans was a prisoner, fast in his prison cell,*
> *And those who read about his crime, they damned his soul to hell.*
> *Saying go down you murderers, go down.*
> *For the murder of his own true wife, and the killing of his own child,*
> *The jury found him guilty and the hanging judge he smiled.*
> *They moved him out of C-Block to his final flowery dell,*
> *And day and night two screws were there and they never left his cell.*

Second, *Who Killed Davey Moore?*, a song by Boy Bylan about another death:

> *Who killed Davey Moore? Not I said the boxing writer, pounding his print on his old typewriter,*
> *Says boxing ain't to blame, there's just as much danger in a football game,*
> *Says boxing's here to stay, it's just the old American way.*
> *Who killed Davey Moore? Not I said the man whose fist laid him low in a cloud of mist,*
> *Who came here from Cuba's shore where boxing ain't allowed no more,*
> *I hit him, yes it's true, but that's what I was paid to do.*
> *Don't say murder, don't say kill, it was destiny, it was God's will.*

This, I would have thought, was a more authentic voice for the 'sixties.

The paradoxical situation of a generation of folk-singers neglecting what is the precise duty of the folk-singer—to document the events and feelings of his time in the music of his time—was well expressed by a young American singer, Dick Farina: 'Folk music, through no active fault of its own, fooled us into certain sympathies and nostalgic allegiances with the so-called traditional past. The Thirties. The Highways and the Open Roads. The Big West . . . Labour Unions. Childe Ballads.' Yes, and in this country one could add the Dignity of Labour, the Mines and the Railroads. Occasionally our folk-singers have covered vital subjects like the Bomb and capital punishment, and all praise to them for this, whatever the quality of the resulting songs. But at the same time they have ignored vast areas of the fabric of contemporary life in Britain, and especially those areas where they might have most chance of reaching a wider public. This doesn't mean pampering to popular taste: there could be a wealth of spiky comment in songs which looked at hire-purchase living, the Mod-Rocker battles, drug taking, the Pill, the James Bond ethos, advertising and, as Kenneth Allsop once delightfully put it, 'Being turned down by Sussex ("One A-level too few, they say-hey-hey-hey-haid").'

'My Black Cadillac With Them White-wall Tyres' (Lightnin' Hopkins)

For all its shortcomings and obstinate roots in the past, the new folk-music provided one of the bases on which the folk/pop amalgam was built. Most importantly, it established a nuclear audience who were concerned that *some* popular music should be serious.

The influences that were to help to transport folk, briefly and abortively, into the 'sixties and the Hit Parade, began to take shape almost simultaneously in Britain and America. In Britain it was the upsurge of a home-grown rhythm and blues.

It has been one of the more curious paradoxes of recent pop history that dance music from the negro ghettoes should have become so popular amongst affluent white teenagers. A few British groups—notably Alexis Korner's Blues Incorporated—had been playing this up-beat urban blues music since the early 'sixties. Their audiences were devoted but small, and could only be found in jazz club areas where there was already an interest in negro music. But when the Beatles sprang a diluted and cheerfully anglicized version of this sound upon the public, interest in rhythm and blues snowballed. The bulk of the combinations that made it during the ensuing Great Group Rush could be loosely described as r. and b. (Just how loosely can be ascertained by comparing them with a genuine Chicago night-spot article like Muddy Waters.) The Rolling Stones, the Yardbirds, Manfred Mann, the Pretty Things and the Animals all use the chunky, insidious guitar sound and curling harmonica wail that are characteristic of the city blues. (Though more recently the pattern in instrumentation has moved closer to jazz: most of the groups now include an organ, and the Alan Price Set, the Graham Bond Organization, and Georgie Fame and the Blue Flames all use saxes in the front line.)

In the clubs the bulk of the material which these groups play is by negro artists. The more primitive groups which lack melody instruments will use Bo Diddley and Jimmy Reed songs; and the more sophisticated, numbers by Jimmy Smith, James Brown and B. B. King. But on record they will frequently produce original numbers which have been written in the r. and b. idiom (but which—if you are bothered about authenticity—are not *really* rhythm and blues). As we shall see later, some of these songs—for instance the Stones' *Satisfaction*, the Animals' *We Gotta Get Out of This Place*, and Manfred Mann's *Why Bother?*—came close to having the same sort of strength and directness in their lyrics as many original blues. As the singer, Rod Stewart, once oracularly remarked, it is as easy to have the blues in the Archway Road as on a deep south railway.

But it was the image and sound of British r. and b., rather than its lyrics, which were to be its chief contribution to the forging of 'protest music'. After an era in which Cliff Richard had been voted Boyfriend of the Year, and described by Colin MacInnes as 'every mother's cherished adolescent son' it was something of a relief when the new breed began trooping to the dock on drunkenness, smuggling and paternity charges. None of this endeared beat musicians to the older generation, but at least is showed they weren't made of celluloid. Typically, though, the basically conformist teenage audience gave most approval to the more superficial signs of rebellion: the shoulder-length hair, the cool, incipiently aggressive stances on stage, and the extravagant clothes. Adults, to discourage their children, affected outrage. 'Would you let your daughter marry a Rolling Stone?' asked one flip journalist. In solidarity, the waiters of the country gave their answer, and ejected the Stones from their hotels for not wearing ties.

These were merely some of the symptoms of the revolution through which the pop world was passing in 1963. Class barriers were breaking down, and the Beatles' twin virtues of musical toughness and anarchic integrity had helped to encourage into pop many people who had previously been contemptuous of its feebleness and sham respectability. Middle-class bohemians who had been playing the blues at parties for years, and growing their hair for even longer, suddenly found themselves on television. One of the most uncompromising groups, the Pretty Things, had a hit record called *Don't Bring Me Down*, which was rife with beatnik philosophy and junkie innuendo:

> *I'm on my own, just wanna roam.*
> *I'll tell you man, don't want a home,*
> *I wander round, feet off the ground,*
> *Diggin' sounds from town to town.*
> *I say I think this life is grand,*
> *I say, I dig it man, don't bring me down, man,*
> *Don't bring me down.*

As the astute Negro writer LeRoi Jones put it, writing of British rhythm and blues groups:

> They take the style (energy, general form, etc.) of black blues country or city, and combine it with the visual image of white American non-conformity . . . and score heavily. These English boys . . . have actually made a contemporary form, unlike most white U.S. 'Folk singers' who are content to imitate 'ancient' blues forms and older singers, arriving at a kind of popular song, at its most hideous in groups like Peter, Paul and Mary.[1]

There is something persistently contemporary about the

[1] *Down Beat* 32, 25 March, 1965.

blues that makes it a more legitimate form to extend in this way than the industrial ballad or the rural folk-song. In the case of classical, rural blues this is no doubt a result of the timeless imprint they carry of their singers' own experiences and fantasies. But it is also true of relatively modern city blues: unless you are an expert you will find great difficulty in dating a Muddy Waters or John Lee Hooker recording. This is more surprising, because city blues, or rhythm and blues, is conventionally a group product that is played solely for dancing.

But if it has few pretensions at being a vehicle for personal statements, rhythm and blues has clearly caught something of the *mood* of the urban negro and the tone of city life. This can perhaps explain why it has been so easily assimilated by British teenagers, and why the early British rhythm and blues of 1963 shows little sign of giving away its age, in contrast to every other type of pop music of that year. Certainly the Elephant and Castle mod has much in common with the young jive-talking Chicago negro. They are both on the way up, breaking free of a legacy of obscurity, discrimination, and physical and mental undernourishment.

The very sound of rhythm and blues is symbolic of this new attitude. The bent, sliding guitar notes and the relentless ratchet beat of the drums demands from performer and dancer—and even mere listener—a certain subjective posture, almost a way of holding the muscles. You will see this expressed again in the way young people walk: cool, easy and detached. It is very much a posture of our time, a combination of ambition, cynicism and unsentimentality.

Many of the elements of the modern negro singer's mythology are shared by the hip white teenager, for instance, those concerning the social and symbolic status of the automobile. Chuck Berry, Bo Diddley and Lightnin' Hopkins all show in their songs what amounts to an obsession with the motor car. Chuck Berry's *No Particular Place to Go* is the whimsical tale of a couple who have to drive right through their date because of a safety-belt jam. Bo Diddley and many others have used the automobile as a sexual metaphor:

I'm a road runner, honey, and you can't keep up with me.
Oh yeh, you say you fast, but it don't look like you gonna
last. (*Road Runner*)

(The car seems to have become a symbol of victory for the negro, an insignia of success in the white man's own terms. The legendary Highway 61, a concrete hypodermic that used to be one of the main migratory routes for negroes fleeing the South during the Depression, now hums with their Chevys and Ford Mustangs.)

The Civil Rights struggle has played much the same role in rejuvenating American folk-music as C.N.D. did in modernizing British folk-song. The initial situations were almost exactly parallel. America, like England, had an upsurge of apolitical folk-music in the late 'fifties. In the Universities, particularly, there was enormous interest in the cheeful and refined skiffling of groups like the Kingston Trio. Then, dramatically, American students started to develop a political conscience. Large numbers of them began to take part in the freedom-rides and sit-ins organized by negro activists in the Southern states. Others helped organize relief work in the ghettoes of the North. Early in 1965 there was a massive student uprising at Berkely, California, that made world-wide news and almost brought the University to a standstill. Ostensibly the revolt was about the quality of teaching on the campus, but underneath one could detect a far-reaching attack on the whole nature of American society, on its materialism, its hypocrisy and its self-righteousness.

Folk-singers fitted into this ferment as easily as badges on a duffel coat. At demonstrations they would lead the singing of *We Shall Overcome* as the protesters were carried off to the police wagons. Spirituals like this, many of them conceived generations ago to help the negro believe in his eventual triumph over slavery, transposed easily and pointedly to the tear-gas-filled streets of Alabama.

The song writers that were thrown up by this new radical movement, like Dick Farina and Phil Ochs, gave their best work back to it. Thankfully they were quite without the puritanism that had plagued the British folk revival. There was even a rumour that on the historic march to Selma some of them had carried Sony transistor televisions so as not to miss the Tamla-Motown show. With the backing, too, of the long tradition of the blues, on whose behalf they were in a sense struggling, they were able to write songs of far greater strength and contemporariness than anything that came out of this country during the equivalent period. Dylan's famous *Blowin' In The Wind*, for instance, had the sort of rich mongrelization—of ballad with blues with spiritual—that could only be a product of a cultural mixing-palette like the New World.

> *Yes, and how many times must a man look up*
> *Before he can see the sky?*
> *Yes, and how many ears must one man have*
> *Before he can hear people cry?*
> *Yes, and how many deaths will it take till he knows*
> *That too many people have died?*
> *The answer, my friend, is blowin' in the wind,*
> *The answer is blowin' in the wind.*[1]

Then, late in 1964, the Americans began their 'involvement' in Vietnam, and student radicalism reached a new high point, with some young men facing long prison sentences by burning their draft cards in front of the television cameras. By the summer of 1965 the first protest songs were beginning to show their angry faces on the British pop scene.

It would be facile and misleading to suggest that these events were the direct and sole causes of the protest craze. No social or cultural trend, however slight, can be explained so easily. Yet most of the protest singers did come from the British and American folk-singing camps, most of their songs were played with an r. and b. backing, and most of the lyrics (initially at least) were concerned, either explicitly or implicitly, with the Vietnam War and racial injustice. I have discussed the background in detail to show just how far the roots of protest music were 'of the people'.

[1] This, and all subsequent Bob Dylan lyrics are copyright Blossom Music Ltd.

It would be equally facile to declare a simple causal relation between the invasion of the commercial pop scene by these up-beat political folk-songs and their rapid deterioration. Instead, I shall merely describe what happened in rough chronological order.

The first obvious landmark was raised when the Manfred Mann group played Dylan's *With God On Our Side* on *Ready, Steady, Go!* Dylan was already in the wind in this country, having made two live visits and a lot of L.P.s. But apart from inoffensive numbers like *Don't Think Twice It's All Right* his songs were not widely known outside folk-music circles.

With God On Our Side was a bitter satire on the habit common amongst generals and politicians of invoking God's support to justify their actions.

> *I can't think for you, you'll have to decide,*
> *Whether Judas Iscariot had God on his side.*

The Manfred Mann group had included this song on one of their E.P.s, with Dylan's simple guitar accompaniment replaced by an organ-dominated group sound, which built up to a powerful climax but never obtruded over the singing. When their vocalist, Paul Jones (once a member of the Oxford Committee of 100), sang this version on *R.S.G.*, it was received tumultuously.

But it was difficult not to be sceptical. What was the applause for? A good song? A sensitive performance? For famous Manfred Mann? Or just for fun, because *R.S.G.* was a live-wire show, and if you didn't clap and cheer the temperature would drop? One could not get rid of a nagging doubt that, if the group had sung a number in favour of the saturation bombing of China, the reaction might have been exactly the same. Not that the sincerity of Paul Jones' powerful performance was ever in doubt: it was as deeply felt as Dylan's original, and musically even stronger. But the sincerity of the audience's response *was*.

With God On Our Side set a pattern, in more ways than one. Although Joan Baez was allowed to sing her sweeter version late one night on B.B.C. television, the song was conspicuously absent from all other B.B.C. channels. When questioned about this, the Corporation said that the reason was the absence of any requests for it. Which was difficult to believe, since the E.P. which contained it was in the Top Twenty.

Sonny and Cher, the next happening, were hardly protest singers. But their unique husband-and-wife act seemed to be part of the pop scene's groping towards reality. They were a strange looking couple: Sonny—short, sad, clownish; Cher—tall, dark-eyed, long-haired and clad always in bell-bottom trousers. Their Number One hit, *I've Got You Babe*, was a typically trite love song. But the way they sang it—*to* each other—had a certain childish sincerity about it.

Unfortunately the honesty was at the level of a remark which Cher made about her husband in the *Music Echo*: 'I love him for everything he is and has been to me . . . from his long hair to his funny shoes.'[1] This depth of feeling was not enough to survive the ruthless march of fashion, and within six months Sonny and Cher had been forgotten.

The two records which really established protest as a fashion were Donovan's *Universal Soldier* and Barry MacGuire's *Eve of Destruction*, both of which entered the Hit Parade in September 1965. Donovan belonged, stylistically, to the folk-music scene, and had eased his way gently into the pop world as a result of four highly successful appearances on *Ready, Steady, Go!* After that the full accolades due to the pop singer were heaped upon him: mentions in the gossip columns, interviews in the pop music papers, and full publicity coverage from Pye.

At the beginning of his career, Donovan was often dismissed as a second-rate imitation of Dylan. In truth, there was a certain physical similarity between these two Puckish boys, with their curly, ragamuffin hair and frail figures. And at this stage they both accompanied themselves on acoustic guitars. But there could scarcely have been more difference in the mood of their songs. Dylan was tough and cynical and, even at his most critical, very, very American. His early songs, and the language he ribbed them with, came straight out of the desolate concrete landscape of down-town New York.

Donovan was a product of the Cornwall beat scene, that

[1] 25 December, 1965.

rather sad menage of young people who hoped that by opting out of society to the tranquillity of St Ives and Newquay they could discover how to love and understand one another. Most of Donovan's own compositions show the same romantic naïvety, and suffer from over-worked naturalistic metaphors of sea, sun and wind. 'Logic,' he said in an interview in the *TV Times*, just before a perceptive Rediffusion documentary on his life, 'I can do without'. It was no surprise when he turned up a few weeks later at a prediction party given by the astrologer, Maurice Woodruff. But, for all this, love songs like *Catch the Wind* and *Josie* have a wistful charm and a consistency of personal style, and these are rare qualities in pop music.

Universal Soldier was the title track from an E.P. of anti-war songs that reached the high position in the Hit Parade (for an E.P.) of number eleven. It was not in fact written by Donovan, but by the American singer, Buffy St Marie, who showed with this song and others like *Till It's Time For You To Go* that she is one of the very best contemporary songwriters.

> *He's five-foot-two and he's six-feet-four,*
> *He fights with missiles and with spears.*
> *He's all of thirty-one and he's only seventeen,*
> *He's been a soldier for a thousand years . . .*
> *And he's fighting for Canada, he's fighting for France,*
> *He's fighting for the U.S.A.,*
> *And he's fighting for the Russians and he's fighting for Japan,*
> *And he thinks we'll put an end to war this way.*
> *And he's fighting for democracy, he's fighting for the Reds,*
> *He says it's for the peace of all.*
> *He's the one who must decide who's to live and who's to die,*
> *And he never sees the writing on the wall . . .*
> *He's the one who gives his body as a weapon of the war,*
> *And without him all this killing can't go on.*

When the B.B.C. obligingly allowed this to be played on all their services, the rationale behind their unofficial censorship policies became murky beyond comprehension.

But if everyone was given a fair chance to hear the record, this was no guarantee of its being *listened* to. When *Universal Soldier* was played on Radio London, it was punctuated by shrieks and gun-noises from the disc jockeys. During its spell in the Hit Parade, I saw servicemen listening to it on juke-boxes with what appeared to be pleasure. And when Donovan's name began featuring in advertisements for toothpaste, there was good reason to doubt if any of his songs were communicating in the way he intended.

Are you a Donofan? Folknik sweetie, profile slurred in cigarette-smoke, how does your garden grow in the magic land of Folk? For you, is one-name Donovan just the job or do you save up sighs for Dylan (Bob)? Whatever sort of folk you dig, of this be sure, that dreaming face in cloudy shock of soft-brushed hair, needs Gordon Moore's, the modern cosmetic toothpaste that tints your gums a pink that sings, shines teeth as bright as guitar strings.

Barry McGuire's *Eve of Destruction*, written by P. F. Sloane, was a very different song to *Universal Soldier*. McGuire's croaking, desperate voice, and the tumultuous beat backing, made it undeniably exciting. But its message was nihilistic and confused, a flamboyant poster for every instant protest cliché.

> *Think of all the hate there is in Red China,*
> *Then take a look around to Selma, Alabama.*
> *You may leave here for four days in space,*
> *But when you return it's the same old place;*
> *The pounding of the drums, the pride and disgrace!*
> *You can bury your dead, but don't leave a trace!*
> *Hate your next-door neighbour, but don't forget to say*
> *grace!*
> *And you tell me, over and over again, my friend;*
> *Ah, you don't believe we're on the eve of destruction.*

One feels a certain reluctance to judge *Eve of Destruction* too harshly. In contrast to most pop songs its lyrics did say something, and did express a sort of personal viewpoint. (Though by making them conspicuous and substantial it invited the sort of criticism that would be irrelevant, aimed at the conventionally vacuous pop song, where the words are a vehicle for a singer, not an opinion.)

But *Eve* was really little more than grapeshot, the first words rolled off a not very clear-thinking tongue. Its pessimism was unfairly criticised: no writer is under any obligation to offer solutions to the problems he portrays. But dissent is never convincingly communicated by generalized statement, nor anger by Jimmy Porter splutterings. Suspicions about the writer and performer's integrity were increased when Barry McGuire visited this country as a result of his record reaching the Number Four spot. He was delighted that the B.B.C. had banned *Eve of Destruction*: 'I read somewhere that this sort of ban is the new way to get a hit in England.'[1]

And it was hardly a serious-minded radical who took part in the following exchange on Radio London's Marquee Show:[2]

D.J.: Are you as rebellious as you sound on your records:
B.M.: Yes, I'm very rebellious.
D.J.: Will you growl for me?
Barry McGuire obliged.

By October there were a dozen or more songs in the Top Fifty which were being filed under 'protest', simply because nothing quite like them had occurred in pop music before. There was the Hollies' *Too Many People*, a song about over-population, which ended with the roar of an H-bomb explosion. One of the Hollies explained:

It kind of says that God has ways of cutting down the population when there really are too many people in the world.
War does away with a lot, and then there were things like the Plague of London. It kinds of levels things up.[3]

Their recording manager levelled things up a bit more by saying:

I suppose it will be controversial, but that never did any harm. It's publicity, and with a record you're just selling a product.[4]

[1] *Melody Maker*, 18 September, 1965.   [2] 23 October, 1965.
[3] *New Musical Express*, 24 September, 1965.   [4] Ibid.

Then there was Sonny's (of Sonny and Cher) *Laugh at Me*, a rather dismal piece of self-pity which he wrote after being ejected from a restaurant because of his appearance. But perhaps the worst of all was a number written by Jonathan King for Hedgehoppers Anonymous.

It's good news week, someone's dropped a bomb somewhere
Contaminating atmosphere and blackening the sky . . .

Good News Week was glib enough in its own right, but appeared doubly offensive when it was revealed that the singers were a group from, of all institutions, the R.A.F.[1]

By now, complaints about the craze were coming as fast as the songs themselves. 'Sing a song of protest—and you, too, could find yourself there in the charts,'[2] said a writer in the *New Musical Express*. Paul McCartney, who had worn a C.N.D. badge in his younger days, complained: 'Well, the songs are all getting a bit silly, aren't they? . . . Protest songs make me concentrate too much on the lyric, which I don't like.'[3]

This feeling was echoed in a remark in the show-pages of *Parade*, which was typical of the reactions of the popular press:

What *about* all this folk song stuff getting mixed up with protest and message songs? How do you feel about it? Do you really think that the messages get over?

I have a hunch that the youngsters hardly even hear the some-what corny lyrics. Anyway, when Peter, Paul and Mary arrive and say that their aim is to 'save the world' with their songs I give up.

Why don't they just get on with the business of entertaining with their songs and earning good money, like they did the other

---

[1] There is something in the nature of pop music that makes it much more important that a singer means what he sings than that an actor means what he acts. Perhaps this is because the songwriter—unlike the playwright—has a very low status in the mythology of pop, and the performer is thought of, rightly or wrongly, as being the real creator.
[2] Alan Smith, 24 September, 1965.
[3] *Melody Maker*, 2 October, 1965.

night in a Jack Benny T.V. show (in which I could detect no
message that could save the world!).

What with Joan Baez saying she regarded herself as a politician
more than a singer, and Donovan sounding off here, there and
everywhere, it seems to me that the young warblers are getting a
shade too uppity.[1]

In this case there was some justification for the tone of this
journalist's remarks. But they also contained a compact sum-
mary of most of the attitudes with which the operators shackle
pop: the assumption that pop music's only function is to entertain, and that it is impossible for songs with a 'message' to
do this; that young people should not criticise society, particularly if they are making money; above all, the total lack of
discrimination, the grouping of Joan Baez and Donovan with
all the other protest singers, as if there were no differences in
their sincerity and skill.

By December 1965 the protest fashion had expired, deflated
by a surfeit of irrelevant and misleading publicity, an audience
that was, as usual, getting bored, and the influx of a large number of spurious songs. If the B.B.C. banned most of these (whilst
allowing plays and films on identical subjects) because they
believed that it was all but impossible to communicate honestly
in a pop song, then they probably reasoned correctly. (Though
this doesn't of course justify their bans.) Even when the
audience listened and understood, it could be an unreal,
vicarious appreciation, a substitute for conscience instead of a
prelude to it. As Philip Oakes once remarked, 'You, too, can
be a liberal: all you have to do is play the record.'

The influence of protest has lingered on in a number of
songs, which are refreshing only because of the personalization
and comparative novelty of their themes. Normally their value,
as well as their content, can be judged by the swiftest look at
their titles: *If You Want Me Take Me For What I'm Worth,
Can't Help Thinking About Me, A Young Girl of Sixteen* ('lying

[1] *Parade,* 23 October, 1965.

there by the road'), and *We Didn't Ask to be Brought Here.*
But simultaneously a separate strand of comment music has
been evolving, the more convincing because the performers
involved are not making a conscious, deliberate effort to be
controversial or committed. Admittedly groups like the Rolling
Stones, the Yardbirds and the Animals are sufficiently well-
known to be able to afford to sing what they like. But this
doesn't detract from the fact that these three groups have
already begun to create an indigenous tradition of tough, contemporary and astringently witty songs.

It's a pity that Mick Jagger is rarely able to make his voice
intelligible over the Stones' backing, for the lyrics of the
group's own compositions are usually very good indeed.
Nineteenth Nervous Breakdown, for instance, was about a
neurotic deb; *Spider and the Fly,* about the sort of girl that
beat musicians were prone to find next to them in clubs:

> *She told me later she was a machine operator*
> *She said she liked the way I held the microphone.*

Perhaps mention ought also to be made of the Who, a less
substantial group, but with their twitchy, anxious style an
authentic voice for the mod cult. Their most celebrated hit,
My Generation, had a certain brazen honesty about it, but was
chiefly remarkable for the singer's well-affected stutter
('P-p-p-p-people try to put us down'). The Who explained this
as being symbolic of the inarticulateness of the working-class
teenager. More impudent commentators let it slip that they
had heard the same voice defect in Wardour Street on Sunday
mornings, as the mods were working off their amphetamine
hangovers.

But if there is one group whose music is likely to survive as
being truly representative of the nineteen sixties, I would guess
it would be the Animals. Their unashamed rock'n'roll has an
honesty and depth of feeling that is rare in British pop. All the
grime and guts of their home town, Newcastle, come across in
their performance, and their singer, Eric Burdon, has something
of the aura of a modern gangster hero: narrow-eyed, hard-
living, and openly fond of money.

The Aftermath: December, 1966

Nineteen sixty-six has not been without incident in the world of pop music; Cliff Richard had lunch at The Athenaeum; Donovan found himself; Little Richard held a nostalgic rockers' convention at the Saville Theatre, the rockers attending in drape jackets and crepe-soled shoes, Little Richard dressing his hair in the style of Shirley Temple and bringing his mother.

That wasn't all. Mick Jagger appeared on the Eamonn Andrews Show and astounded viewers by talking in real sentences; Paul Jones was heard discussing literary works on the radio; pop singers in interviews said they were reading the works of Huxley, Sartre and Dr Timothy Leary. One even claimed to be reading *Ulysses*—a far cry from *The Catcher in the Rye*, which was Adam Faith's intellectual fodder for so long.

Donovan did his best to replace P. J. Proby who, alas, dis-disappeared without trace—Tom Jones bow, Dobermann Pinscher and all.

But there were compensatory laughs. There was a psychedelic happening at the Albert Hall with shots of London buses and bubbles and old cinema intermission lights. Andrew Oldham said Scott Engel of the Walker Brothers was the Joan Crawford of pop music, and Scott Walker said no he wasn't—he was the Greta Garbo. The *Sunday Telegraph* described Andrew Oldham as the Rolling Stones' 'creative manager'.

Any pop singer, at a loss for something to say, said he was thinking of opening a boutique. (As Clement Freud so rightly pointed out, one feels such a fool without a boutique nowadays.)

Many grew moustaches to cheer themselves up: the Beatles grew moustaches, so did the occasional Rolling Stone, and the odd Holly and Kink.

Dead soldiers' clothes became fashionable for stage and leisure wear. So did producing records, writing plays and discovering people—anything rather than the actual singing. Mick Jagger took to producing: 'Jagger,' said an admirer, 'who brought Nureyev to rock'n'roll is now the Zeffirelli of pop.' We saw the story of Donovan's life on television: 'My job,' he said, 'is writing beautiful things about beauty. You see, my life is beautiful.'

The smartest way of getting about was in a Mini Cooper S with black windows, though long night journeys were accomplished in Rolls-Royces (two Beatles, one Stone), Bentley Continentals (one Stone, Brian Epstein) or Mercedes saloons (one Rolling Stone)—all with black windows. 'I am thinking,' said Paul McCartney tartly, 'of getting a bicycle with black windows.' (It was quite a game to see how far you could get inside the gates of Buckingham Palace in your Rolls-Royce.)

The Beatles ceased to be the Famous Four in the musical papers; they were respectfully referred to as the Young Millionaires.

Nervous exhaustion was all the rage. Scott Engel was exhausted nervously; so was a Kink, a Yardbird and a Cream. Mick Jagger was reported to be nervously exhausted after buying furniture for his new flat. There were little displays of artistic temperament; the usual spitting cases were out, and in the last few months even nervous exhaustion was on the decline.

It was replaced by the conviction that everything was beautiful, groovy and gentle. Pop singers floated round loving people in a patronising manner that was even more infuriating than their protest songs. 'When you are aware,' Donovan said, 'there are no such things as hate and envy: there is only love.'

'This industry of human happiness,' said Andrew Oldham crossly.

Oh yes, there were laughs in plenty; but nothing could disguise the fact that the pop scene that has diverted the general public for the last three years is over, finished and done with. 'Ready Steady Gone' said the backcloth on the last programme, and it was the end of an era.

Paradoxically, the records are better than ever: the Who, the Kinks, the Hollies, the Beatles, the Stones and the Beach Boys have produced some splendid things; but the vigour, the freshness and the monstrous nerve have gone. Val Doonican and the Seekers at the top of the hit parade is not without significance; it marks the return of the dreaded all-round entertainer, the triumph of Tin Pan Alley. Mr Leslie Perrin, a most respected publicity agent, now does publicity for the Rolling Stones—a group whose early appeal was founded on the rumour that they didn't wash.

The end was inevitable. Excitement exhausts the public; they can get steamed up only so often. There is therefore no point in looking for new Beatles for at least another six years, during which time we can enjoy the timeless charm of *Juke Box Jury*, and those dreary American television idols, Batman, Napoleon Solo and Illya Kuryakin.

The pop singers themselves have grown old; their faces on television look old, world-weary; bored faces that have seen it all. The future is bleak—just as those pre-Beatle years were bleak—but the present, while they sort themselves out, is pretty sordid.

Nineteen sixty-six is the year the whole thing turned sour. Many found they hadn't made the money they ought to have made. The shock reduced them to complete inactivity. Managers could not get them to work at all in the industry of human happiness. They sat at home having beautiful and groovy thoughts about life, and entertaining grandiose notions about themselves.

Many groups broke up, fighting about who would be first and who would be last; the Animals scattered, Chris Curtis left the Searchers, Georgie Fame abandoned his Blue Flames, and Yardbirds still issue statements to fans once a week. 'It's just as well,' said one manager, 'that there are so few television programmes for them. They look dreadful close up, loathing each other.' (No sign, as yet, of a rift in the Bachelors—heartening news.)

What, one wonders, will happen to them? They can't all be absorbed by boutiques. Will they—and this seems Brian Epstein's policy—all go into pantomime? Or will they—which is what the richer ones do at the moment—stay in retirement, cut off from the world in their large houses, making home movies and having beautiful and groovy thoughts, far removed from the industry of human happiness?

The best records this year have been *Eleanor Rigby*, *Yellow Submarine*, and almost all the tracks on the Beatles' LP, *Revolver*. Paul McCartney, seemingly without effort, produced song after song of aching beauty. *River Deep Mountain High* was a good record; also *Substitute* by the Who, and that perfectly extraordinary composition by Ray Davies of the Kinks, *Dead End Street*. 'What are we living for?' he cries in that lifeless voice of his, What indeed? I also liked *God Only Knows* and *Sloop John B.* by the Beach Boys: and *Mrs Applebee* and *Bus Stop*.

There were some really bad records—more notably Cher's *Mama, What Happens When My Dollies Have Babies?* (she may well ask). Bobby Darin had a huge success with *If I Were a Carpenter*. Not surprisingly: the combination of utterly meaningless words with the most meaningful voice was always a winner. And I liked the subjunctive.

The smartest pop singer was, first, Mick Jagger, who had his portrait painted by Cecil Beaton, but by the end of the year it was the Beatles. They became unbearably smart. Unlike anybody else, they seemed to know what they wanted.

George went to Bombay for 10 weeks to learn the sitar; it was rumoured that his wife, Pattie, was learning belly dancing. 'It's going to be great round at George's,' say his friends. Smartest of all was Paul, now known in the musical world as The Trendy Beatle or 'a very happening person'. He commissioned Peter Blake to copy Landseer's Monarch of the Glen.

Paul also summed up the pop singer's attitude to the written note. 'It doesn't look like music to me,' he said.

And Donovan said 'Gipsy Dave and I are the closest you can get in friendship without a bed'.

And Andrew Oldham said: 'This is the year of the crucifixion and only some of us have managed to pull the nails out of our fingers. Few will survive.'

And George Harrison said: 'If we do slip, so what? Who cares? We'll be just where we were, only richer. Being a Beatle isn't the living end.'

Just fine as long as it lasts.[1]

Bob Dylan

It's difficult to know how to do justice to an artist as complex and prolific as Dylan without giving him a disproportionate amount of attention. If the reader considers that the following pages are too many to devote to one artist, I can only plead that Dylan's career has been a pageant in which the whole functional crisis of pop has been acted out. Because, too, he is a poet as well as a pop singer, the enactment has been coloured in explosive and extravagant detail, rife with subtlety and contradiction. No story animates more pointedly the basic dilemma of modern popular art: how to be creative and still satisfy a mass audience.

To elaborate on his status as a songwriter, I can do no better than break my normal rule and quote a slightly earlier article than usual.

[1] Maureen Cleave, 'The Year Pop Went Flat' in *Evening Standard*, 29 December, 1966.

December, 1964

The appearance of Bob Dylan's fourth LP record[1] seems an appropriate occasion to cease regarding him merely as a phenomenon (though he remains that) and to consider seriously his achievement as an artist.

Insofar as Dylan's musicianship is concerned, there can be little room for reservation. His first album (*Bob Dylan*), consisting mostly of standard blues arranged by him, left no doubt as to his real talent, which is original, distinctive, and at the same time based firmly in the tradition. At the age of twenty, when he made this 1961 recording, Dylan was already a 'professional' in the highest sense. His rendering of the blues, *Fixin' to Die* and *See that My Grave is Kept Clean,* has an uncanny resemblance to the originals, and his tribute to Woody Guthrie (one of two of his own songs on this record) sounds like a younger version of Guthrie himself.

As one is bound increasingly to realise, listening to Dylan, it is his incredible ear for what has gone before him that gives his own songs their deep roots in the tradition and makes them as 'authentic' as they are. This is not to imply a slavish imitation. Indeed, one of the more striking aspects of Dylan's first album is the way he departs from the usual style in which such songs as *Gospel Plow* and *Pretty Peggy-O* are sung. So radical is his treatment, that they become virtually new songs with him; but even their newness is realised within the broad contours of a tradition. It is this dual quality of rootedness and unhesitant readiness to depart along his own distinctive path that is the substance of Dylan's art.

Dylan's second album (*The Freewheelin' Bob Dylan*), which contains the enormously popular *Blowin' in the Wind,* offers further evidence of his mastery of the technique and tradition necessary to strike out in exciting new directions without losing his substance in superficial gimmickry. His assimilation of the blues style and outlook shows up especially well in his faultless, if unconventional, version of *Don't Think Twice,* and his own blues, *Down the Highway.* The latter piece is particularly interesting because of the success with which he has translated his own blues experience (occasioned by the departure of his girl for Italy) into the Negro idiom.

[1] *Another Side of Bob Dylan,* CBS, BPG 62429.

F

Dylan's understanding of the blues goes a long way towards explaining his success as a songwriter in his own right: 'The way I think about the blues comes from what I learned from Big Joe Williams. . . . What made the real blues singers so great is that they were able to state all the problems they had; but at the same time, they were standing outside of them and could look at them. And in that way, they had them beat. What's depressing today is that many young singers are trying to get inside the blues, forgetting that those older songsters used them to get outside their troubles.'

One recognizes in these words, of course, not merely a truth about the blues, but about art itself. Being inside and outside as experience, the dependence of the tragic and comic not on the material as such but on the direction of the artistic perspective—these are themes of the conflict between classic and romantic aesthetics, and it is this very tension which provides art with its substantive power and insight.

Dylan's art has this tension, for Dylan himself does not simply remain 'outside' his experience as his comment suggests. When he is under the power of his own feeling, as in the strident anger of *Master of War*, he is so in a way that is unsentimental and above all unselfpitying. This lack of sentimentality is strikingly evident in *A Hard Rain's A-Gonna Fall*, 'a desperate kind of song' (notes Dylan) written during the Cuban crisis of 1962. The artistic problems involved in treating such a subject seriously (Dylan has given it a splendid satiric treatment in *Talking World War III Blues*) are seemingly insurmountable; but Dylan has taken long strides in the direction of their solution. He has done so in the only way possible: by employing an approach that is symbolic.

Only a symbolic language could bear the strain of an event as absolute and apocalyptic as the total destruction of life on earth. Dylan's instinctive awareness of the capacities of symbolism is, in this song, turned to brilliant use.

In *Hard Rain*, Dylan has adapted the melody and refrain of the traditional English song, *Lord Randall*, and by this very fact has set his own 'story' in a frame of concreteness:

> *O where have you been, my blue-eyed son,*
> *And where have you been, my darlin' young one?*

But the actual tale which is told in answer to the traditional

question takes place on an altogether different plane of reality
from that of its source:

> *I've stumbled on the side of twelve misty mountains,*
> *I've walked and I've crawled on six crooked highways,*
> *I've stepped in the middle of seven sad forests,*
> *I've been out in front of a dozen dead oceans,*
> *I've been 10,000 miles in the mouths of a graveyard,*
> *And it's a hard, it's a hard, it's a hard, and it's a hard,*
> *It's a hard rain's a-gonna fall.*

The cumulative effect of these images, an effect which is reinforced by the repeated rhythmic figure of the guitar accompaniment, is little short of overwhelming. We are besieged with
images of dead and dying life, a kind of dynamic stasis, a perfect
figurative medium for the vision at the brink:

> *I met a young child beside a dead pony,*
> *I met a white man who walked a black dog,*
> *I met a young woman whose body was burning,*
> *I met a young girl, she gave me a rainbow . . .*

We have the start of many stories here, never to be finished, and
in the very fact of this arrested promise an accurate rendering of
the meaning of that awful apocalypse that may await us. Aptly,
this style, which is so tuned to the reality, was actually dictated by
it. For, as Dylan explains: 'Every line in it (*Hard Rain*) is actually
the start of a whole song. But when I wrote it, I thought I wouldn't
have enough time alive to write all those songs, so I put all I
could into this one'. Because of the precision of the tone and the
adequacy of the statement of the vision, when it is over, and the
respite won, the poet's resolve carries absolute conviction:

> *And I'll tell it and speak it and think it and breathe it,*
> *And reflect from the mountains so all souls can see it,*
> *And I'll stand on the ocean until I start sinkin',*
> *And I'll know my song well before I start singin',*
> *And it's a hard, it's a hard, it's a hard, and it's a hard,*
> *It's a hard rain's a-gonna fall.*

Dylan's third album (*The Times They are A-Changin'*), which
consists entirely of his own compositions, sustains and extends the
high achievement of the second. *Hollis Brown*, which appears on
this disc, is one of the simplest and most effective ballads that

Dylan has written. In it he shows his affinities with the left song-writers of the 'thirties and their concern for the oppressed, but he also manifests the distinguishing characteristics of his own outlook.

Hollis Brown is a South Dakota farmer who shoots his wife and five children to end the misery of their slow starvation (or is it the anguish of his own 'failure'?). This story is so obviously taken from a newspaper account (what writer would risk the crudeness of its invention?) that one need hardly stress the authenticity of its situation and psychology, which are wholly American. There is no solidarity arising from starvation here. Hollis Brown and his family are starving in the interstices of a society which is unaware of their existence.

And this is the fact which fixes the attention of the poet who tells their story: not that they starve amidst plenty (Guthrie's theme in the 'thirties, and still a 'truth' of their plight) but that they are so ultimately alone:

> *The rats have got your flour, bad blood has got your mare.*
> *The rats have got your flour, bad blood has got your mare.*
> *Is there anyone that knows, is there anyone that cares?*
> *You pray to the Lord above, oh please send you a friend.*
> *You pray to the Lord above, oh please send you a friend.*
> *Your empty pockets tell you that you aint a-got no friend.*

The seemingly artless repetition of the word 'friend' weights the term skilfully with its proper emphasis. Indeed, the appearance of simplicity here is deceptive; for, while the elements are few, they are essential. The silence of the Lord above, the speech of empty pockets, the unfound friend—these point to the society which generates Hollis Brown's situation, a society in which the bond which binds things to reality is money, where, if one is moneyless, both the Lord above and friendship are mere figments, divorced from the 'reality' of practical existence.

Technically speaking, *Hollis Brown* is a tour de force. For a ballad is normally a form which puts one at a distance from its tale. This ballad, however, is told in the second person, present tense, so that not only is a bond forged immediately between the listener and the figure of the tale, but there is the ironic fact that the only ones who know of Hollis Brown's plight, the only ones who care, are the hearers who are helpless to help, cut off from him, even as we in a mass society are cut off from each other. The terrible anguish which forces Hollis Brown to the shotgun

on the wall and his desperate solution are powerfully conveyed
by the incessant, driving guitar bass, and by the employment of
images which make one literally feel the tension:

> *Your baby's cryin' louder now, it's a poundin' on your brain.*
> *Your baby's cryin' louder now, it's a poundin' on your brain.*
> *Your wife's screams are stabbin' you, like the dirty drivin' rain.*

That the guitar bass itself should be so suited to the song's
psychological and dramatic purposes is no accident, but proof of
how much Dylan has learned from his teachers. This bass has
strong reminiscences of a bass figure which asserts itself with
insistence in Blind Lemon Jefferson's powerful death blues, *See
That My Grave is Kept Clean*, sung by Dylan in his first album.
Indeed, the blues perspective itself, uncompromising, isolated
and sardonic, is superbly suited to express the squalid reality of
contemporary America. And what a powerful expression it can
be, once it has been liberated (as it has in Dylan's hands) from its
egocentric bondage!

A striking example of the tough, ironic insight one associates
with the blues (and also of the power of understatement which
Dylan has learned from Guthrie) is to be found in the final lines of
Hollis Brown:

> *There's seven people dead on a South Dakota farm.*
> *There's seven people dead on a South Dakota farm.*
> *Somewhere in the distance, there's seven new people born.*

How much of the soul of contemporary American society and its
statistical conscience is expressed in this sardonic image! A more
complex but equally successful Dylan ballad, *The Lonesome Death
of Hattie Carroll*, also appears in this third album. Bearing as
well the earmarks of a newspaper story, this ballad relates the
gratuitous murder of a Negro maid, Hattie Carroll, by a 24-year-
old scion of Maryland society, who strikes her for a minor blunder
at a social gathering and is given a six-month sentence for his
crime. The refrain provides the story with a bitter moral and
political commentary. As the tragedy of Hattie Carroll's life and
death unfolds, it cries:

> *You who philosophise disgrace*
> *And critise our fears*
> *Take the rag away from your face*
> *Now ain't the time for your tears.*

But after the court hands down its 'penalty' the last couplet
changes to:

> *Bury the rag deep in your face*
> *Now's the time for your tears.*

It is not the refrain and commentary, however, but the subtle
embodiment within the story of the terrible bondage of the
American Negro, that makes this ballad the remarkable and
moving achievement that it is:

> *Hattie Carroll was a maid in the kitchen,*
> *She was fifty-one years old and gave birth to ten children,*
> *Who carried the dishes and took out the garbage,*
> *And never sat once at the head of the table,*
> *And didn't even talk to the people at the table,*
> *Who just cleaned up all the food from the table,*
> *And emptied the ashtrays on a whole lotta levels . . .*

This is a tremendously articulate language; with a few, again
seemingly artless strokes, Dylan conveys the tedium, the humilia-
tion, the frustration of this life in servitude. Contrast it with the
portrait he gives of Hattie Carroll's murderer, and you have an
unforgettable and indispensable insight into one level of the
conflict which is at present tearing America apart.

Having dwelt on the triumphs of Dylan's art, it is only proper
to note a shortcoming shared by a number of the less successful
of his songs. This is a tendency to make the song an argument, so
that when we have its 'formula' or 'message', the song loses its
tension, and with that its life. The satire on American patriotism,
With God On Our Side, though not without its satisfactions,
suffers from this defect, as does *Only A Pawn in Their Game*, a
song about the murder of Medgar Evers. Several of Dylan's non-
political songs, too, exhibit a tendency to tell the listener about
their subject, rather than to express it, and make it live.

When all is said, however, one cannot begin to praise enough
the achievement which these second and third albums represent.
In addition to the selections on the third, already mentioned, the
beautiful and superbly handled love dialogue, *Boots of Spanish
Leather*, the rich allegory, *When the Ship Comes In*, and the title
song, *The Times They Are A-Changin'*, are each artistic triumphs
in their own right.

It is thus with real regret that one has to report the failure of

Dylan's newly released fourth album ever to approach the standard set by his other three. With the exception of *It Ain't Me Babe* and *The Chimes of Freedom*, there is not a song on the record that this listener would care to hear twice.

Several reasons for this failure present themselves, but one in particular seems worth discussing. This is the fact that many of the songs, and especially the more serious ones, are unfinished, indeed, barely begun. *Ballad in Plain D*, which relates Dylan's break-up with his girl, is not really a song at all, but only the raw material for a song. One has the feeling, in listening to it, of reading someone else's mail.

> *Myself, for what I did, I can't be excused,*
> *The changes I was goin' through can't even be used.*

This is embarrassingly bad. The problem is that it is not exceptional, and that, while as a lapse it may represent an extreme, it defines the characteristic weakness of the better songs on this record: they are still in the foetal stages of their development.

To offer an explanation for this sudden and unqualified failure of taste and self-critical awareness may appear the height of presumption, but with an art as rich as Dylan's at stake it may not be an altogether futile gesture.

For one obvious line of speculation immediately suggests itself: in a culture in which the driving force of social existence, the pretext for art itself, in commercial, 'silence' is a luxury (and freedom) that few artists can afford. By sheer force of his public success, Dylan has ceased to be 'merely' an artist and has become a commodity, a 'hot property' in current parlance. The pressures on him to produce a fourth album (released punctually for the Christmas rush) must have been terrific. Most artists, to survive at all, have ego to spare; the combination, in this case, could have been fatal.[1]

But Dylan, at this time, had no equal in the whole spectrum of pop music. The candour and poetry of his songs, their disturbing insights into the great dilemmas of the contemporary world, their excitement, their wit, their youth, made him tower above every other post-war singer. And he achieved this whilst—long-haired and be-jeaned—still retaining the

[1] David Horowitz, 'Bob Dylan: Genius or Commodity?' in *Peace News*, 11 December, 1964.

indisputable persona of a pop singer. He was a *genuine* idol: a generator, not of fashions and hair-styles, but of ideals and attitudes.

When he performed before a packed audience in the Festival Hall, London, one beautiful Sunday afternoon in May, 1964, his frail figure hunched in the centre of the stage, he gave off a magnetism that some critics present likened to that of Callas or Segovia.

His two-hour act was a masterpiece of informal theatre as well as of musicianship. He ambled and skipped around the stage, drinking alternately from a glass of water and a giant mug of whiskey; he lost his capo somewhere under the platform and, after minutes of giggling and unsuccessful crawling about, borrowed one from a man in the audience; he interspersed his songs with mumbled, impish cracks about American Society, describing *Inside the Walls of Redwing*, a song about a boys' prison, as his 'school song'.

The rapport which he established with his audience at this concert gave Dylan scope to take expressive liberties with his singing that he could never have got away with on disc. He would slow down a line of a song and stamp in each word with his foot. He would effect preposterous but stunningly felicitous changes in accent, from slangy New York in *Talking World War III Blues* to a pinched, straw-chewing Dakota drawl in *Honey Just Allow Me One More Chance*. And his whole performance was punctuated with wry chuckles, whoops, and bursts of reflective harmonica playing, inserted as if to give the audience time to think. Most memorable of all was the soaring 'No, no, no' chorus-line in *It Ain't Me Babe*, which deliciously, if affectionately, parodied the Beatles' 'Yeah, yeah, yeah'.

But if Dylan's British tour was an unqualified triumph, he himself was unhappy about the way his career was progressing. He was tiring of the protest movement, and of writing songs about society's problems rather than his own. 'I don't want to write *for* people any more,' he said in one interview, 'I want to write from inside me'. He was feeling, too, the stress of living as a pop star, of the constant public exposure, the pressure from reporters to simplify and explain his songs and their significance to a chart-conscious public.

Paradoxically it was Donovan, who had been widely thought of as a surrogate English Dylan (there were even some complaints in the papers that Dylan had copied Donovan!) who first helped the American into the British charts. Columbia records were not blind to Donovan's popularity in this country and, shortly after his four appearances on *R.S.G.*, they released in this country a single record of *The Times they are a-Changin'*, from Dylan's third L.P. of the same name. It was successful enough to reach the Top Twenty. Immediately Dylan was slotted into the current 'protest' craze and persistently interrogated about his political views. In every interview with British reporters, he vehemently denied having any interest in politics or having ever participated in political movements. (Though a friend of his, who writes for the French magazine, *Salut Les Copains*, has said that a considerable proportion of Dylan's earnings goes to left-wing movements in the States.) The degree to which Dylan was affected by being made just another pop scene commodity, to be pigeon-holed and pre-digested by the press, is strikingly revealed by an interview which he gave in *Disc*:

LAURIE HENSHAW   What would you say had been the greatest influence in your life?
BOB DYLAN   You! Your paper happens to influence me a lot. I'm going to go out and write a song after I've seen you—you know—what I'm used for.

I feel what I'm doing and I feel what your paper does. And you have the nerve and gall to ask me what influences me, and why do I think I'm so accepted. I don't want to be interviewed by your paper. I don't need it. You don't need it either.

You can build up your own star. Why don't you just get a lot of money and bring some kid out here from the North of England and say: 'We're gonna make you a star. You just comply with everything we do. Every time you want an interview, you can just sign a paper that means we can have an interview and write what we want to write. And you'll be a star and make money!'

Why don't you just do that? I'm not like that, I'm not going to do it for you.[1]

[1] *Disc*, 22 May, 1965.

Predictably enough, *Disc* relished this attack upon their integrity, and gave the interview banner headlines: 'MR SEND-UP. The most fantastic interview that the amazing Bob Dylan has ever given!' But the mood of Dylan's statement— one of the very few serious interviews he has ever given—can perhaps help to explain why he started to deliberately sabotage the image which the operators had built up of him.

Curiously, there had been an unnoticed warning that this reaction was brewing a whole year before, on the L.P., *The Times they are a-Changin'*. The last track of this record is a song called *Restless Farewell*, in which Dylan viciously attacks the assaults on his privacy that had become one of the consequences of his success. There's no doubt, I think, that one of Dylan's interpretations of privacy is the right to *communicate* privately:

> . . . *not to stand naked under unknowing eyes;*
> *It's for myself and my friends my stories I sing.*

His next L.P. was meaningfully titled *Another Side of Bob Dylan*. (We can trace the whole metamorphosis of Dylan's style in the changing titles of his L.P.s. They are, in chronological order: *Bob Dylan, The Freewheelin' Bob Dylan, The Times they are a-Changin', Another Side of Bob Dylan, Bringing it all back Home, Highway 61 Revisited*.) As David Horowitz points out, this L.P. is a failure by any standards, even the new ones by which Dylan was attempting to free himself from the stereotyped 'protest' image. His versatility is unused, his acid humour diluted down to undergraduate satire level. There is a growing privacy in the lyrics, an introspection that borders on thinking aloud.

In the next two L.P.s this tendency is even more marked. The lyrics become episodic, with verses often as unrelated as random extracts from a surrealist film, and full of symbolism whose imagery is rich but evasive:

> *The motor-cycle black Madonna,*
> *Two-wheeled gipsy queen,*
> *And her silver-studded Phantom*
> *Cause the grey-flanneled dwarf to scream*

As he weeps two wicked birds of prey
Who pick upon his breadcrumb sins.
And there are no sins inside the Gates of Eden.

Evocative as this is, it fails to communicate much beyond a sort of Dylan *angst*, the pervading hallucinogenic despair of being 'hung-up'. In *Ballad of a Thin Man*, a song nominally about an intellectual confronted by a room full of circus freaks, he describes, perhaps inadvertently, what it feels like to be faced with a Dylan song.

You raise up your head, you ask 'Is this where it is?'
And somebody points to you and says 'It's his,'
And you say, 'What's mine?'
And somebody else says 'Well, what is?'
And you say 'My God, am I here all alone?'
But something is happening here and you don't know what
    it is,
Do you, Mr Jones?

But it was Dylan's parallel change of musical style that most outraged his followers. He seemed determined to contradict every feature of the mask which his followers had fashioned for him.

He abandoned, for a start, recording with his own guitar accompaniment, and used instead a tough rhythm and blues backing group. His first single in this style, *Subterranean Home-sick Blues*, was an anarchic nonsense piece that had swing and a great sense of fun. In the States it was sold in a cover that carried a picture of the Beatles. By another artist it would have been unhesitatingly welcomed, but being by Bob Dylan it set off widespread anxiety and shaking of heads. To many it seemed a criminal waste of talent, like Olivier playing in *Dry Rot*. No doubt Dylan himself rocked with pleasure at having upset so many of those who were determined to put boundaries round him. What he failed to realize was that having put out a beat record in a very poppish style, his new mass audience would categorize him just as effectively as any of the image-makers: 'Peculiar, ain't he?' said one girl to me. 'But he's got a lovely smile.'

Dylan's beat backing reduced his flexibility as a performer and in many cases physically obscured his lyrics. But judged on its own terms, his music is inspirational rock'n'roll. And occasionally, in songs such as *Like a Rolling Stone*, he achieved that synthesis between music and lyrics that characterized his earlier numbers. To describe the experience of listening to this song I can only think of the Quaker phrase 'speaking to our condition'.

But in spite of this a great deal had gone from his music. In May 1965 people were camping overnight in the streets outside the Albert Hall in the hope of getting tickets for his second British tour. But the artist the lucky ones saw was a bruised shadow of the one that had been here only twelve months before. The enthusiasm, the wit, the curious mixture of wisdom and innocence, even the enormous versatility of his singing, were scarcely visible. Whatever personal crises helped to cause these changes in Bob Dylan (and, from fairly blatant references in his songs, one can guess what one of them might be), his subjection to the pressures of the pop scene clearly had more than a little to do with it. His future development will be something of a test case; if an artist of his calibre cannot weather these pressures, who can? At his height, the distinguished critic, Ralph Gleason, called him 'One of the great warning voices of our time'. It may turn out that his career will be even more of a warning than his voice.

The New Dylan: a contrary view, March, 1966

Time, if nothing else, will vindicate Bob Dylan's 'New Music' from the sad and even pathetic charges of Social Irresponsibility and Artistic Decadence levelled by the current representatives of the 'thirties and 'forties. Formal excellence and brilliant wit are seldom as appreciated at first glance as are the topical sensations of the hour. Yet *The Hammer Song* and *Banks of Marble* are already dead, while *Mister Tambourine Man*, *Lay Down Your Weary Tune*, and *Chimes of Freedom* become more impressive with each passing year. Bob Dylan requires no extreme rationalization, and his latest and best album no elaborate defence: the evidence of his style and vision is found in his songs.

It is a highly personal style-vision: Dylan's unyielding and poetic point of view represents a total commitment to the subjective over the objective, the microcosm over the macrocosm, man rather than Man, problems not Problems. To put it as simply as possible, the tradition that Dylan represents is that of all great artists: that of projecting, with the highest possible degree of honesty and craftsmanship, a unique personal vision of the world we live in, knowing full well that, unless the personal is achieved, the universal cannot follow. Dylan's historical-political adversaries aren't interested in what one person may see; their myopia recognizes only the sweep of Masses, and they day-dream hopefully of thousands singing union songs in Central Park. From their Disneylandic yearnings, they demand their songs short, snappy, imbecilically simple, and straight to the proletarian point. Thus *Highway 61 Revisited* is considered corrupt and self-indulgent, and Dylan's gloriously ambiguous new works too rich for the People's blood. This is a time for bread, not cake, they rationalize, blissfully unaware that time invariably vindicates form over topicality, and poetry always outlives journalism.

With the advent of *Highway 61 Revisited* (in my opinion, one of the two or three greatest folk music albums ever made), Bob Dylan has exploded, as Leslie Fiedler claims William Burroughs to have 'exploded' the novel, the entire city folk-music scene into the incredibly rich fields of modern poetry, literature, and philosophy; that he did it with his own personal blend of a popular music style, rock-and-roll, is all the more joyful and remarkable. He has, in effect, dragged folk music, perhaps by the nape of the neck, into areas it never dreamed existed, and enriched both it and himself a thousandfold by the journey. Now, for the first time, I think, with this album, we have finally progressed out of Then and into Now. With a Minnesota gypsy leading us, we have truly become contemporary.

Not that it's painless. For Dylan's main concern in *Highway 61 Revisited* is the classic American Dream, Innocence and Experience, a theme that has always haunted and tormented American artists, particularly in the twentieth century. The music of Bob Dylan is the music of illusion and delusion, of men deluded by women, of men and women deluded by surface appearance, a music of the tramp as explorer and the clown as happy victim, where the greatest crimes are lifelessness and the inability to see oneself as circus performer in the show of life. Thus, in *Ballad of a Thin*

Man, Dylan will choose the life of emotion rather than the life of reason: 'You have many contacts among the lumber-jacks to get you facts when someone attacks your imagination.' And again, in *Tombstone Blues*, the outcry against 'useless and pointless knowledge'. In the tender, lovely *Queen Jane Approximately*, Dylan offers some good advice to a popular woman folksinger (but one who 'commissions clowns'). The last verse, to anyone familiar with the New York City folk scene, is brilliant: 'Now when all of the bandits you turn your other cheek to/All lay down their bandannas and complain/And you want somebody you don't have to speak To (my capitals)/Won't you come see me, Queen Jane.'

The charge that Dylan's new songs are vicious, morbid and humourless, and explorations into the death-wish, can be easily repudiated by anyone with a mind to think and an ear to listen. *Highway 61 Revisited* is a corrosively funny satire on the standard businessman-promoter's reply to anything, no matter what, as long as it makes money: 'Why, yes, I think it can be very easily done!' *From a Buick 6* is pure, joyous rock, and a hilarious song. The beautiful *Just Like Tom Thumb's Blues*, with its unforgettable opening lines ('When you're lost in the rain in Juarez when it's Eastertime, too/And your gravity fails and negativity don't pull you through'), is, among other things, a retelling of the old joke of women loving men to death: 'And you're so kind and careful not to go to her too soon/And she takes your voice and leaves you howling at the moon.' And the exquisite *It Takes a Lot to Laugh, It Takes a Train to Cry* is one of the most lyric and bluesy love songs in any tradition or any language.

Desolation Row, a song over eleven minutes long (who else but Dylan could hold attention to a single performance for so long a timespan?), is clearly a major statement. Once again, we are in a dark, Fellini-esque world of clowns and grotesques, but Dylan makes it clear that the tragic man is not the clown *per se*, but the clown who thinks he is something better. Accept the universal truth, Dylan says, accept chaos, and advance from there. We are all child-fools and 'Don't send me no more letters, no, not unless you mail them from Desolation Row'.

The finest song on the album, and Dylan's greatest so far, I think is *Like a Rolling Stone*, the definitive statement that both personal and artistic fulfilment must come, in the main, by being truly on one's own. Dylan's social adversaries have twisted this to mean something very devious and selfish, but that is not the case at all. Dylan is simply kicking away the props to get to the real core of the matter: Know yourself; it may hurt at first, but you'll never get anywhere if you don't. The final 'You're invisible now, you got no secrets to conceal/How does it feel?/How does it Feel?/To be on your own' is clearly optimistic and triumphant, a soaring of the spirit into a new and more productive present.

Much should be said here about the brilliance of Dylan's music itself, of his welding together so many diffuse fragments from so many folk and popular music traditions, of the great musicians who played with him on the album; but there is no space.

Let me close with two things. First, Dylan's own eloquent answer to the social critics: 'I know there're some people terrified of the bomb, but there are other people terrified to be seen carrying a modern screen magazine.' And, finally, from novelist John Clellon Holmes: '(Dylan) has the authentic mark of the bard on him, and I think it's safe to say that no one, years hence, will be able to understand just what it was like to live in this time without attending to what this astonishingly gifted young man has already achieved.[1]

A Synthesis: 1967

Don't be misled because he carries a guitar instead of a quill pen, because he works in a cloud of publicity instead of a garret, because his words are chanted on L.P.s instead of being printed in little magazines. Bob Dylan is a poet, one of the few urgent poets of our time.

If you're at all interested in the excitement of words, all his records are worth buying and his double LP *Blonde On Blonde* (C.B.S. D.D.P. 66012), is essential.

People may tell you that there are two Dylans—the early Dylan who sang about oppressed people straightforwardly, and the new Dylan who sings about his love affairs in a series of flashing images—and that you have to choose between them.

You won't be fooled, you'll choose both. Because there's only one Bob Dylan, and he's big enough to sing about either love or injustice.

Some critics or other, who took up Dylan as a fashion and dropped him in the same way, will tell you that he's become impossibly obscure. Again, you won't be fooled.

[1] Paul Nelson, 'Bob Dylan: Another View' in *Sing Out*, March 1966.

Dylan's songs are complicated. So's the world. Don't expect to take in everything he's handing out the first or even the fourth time. (Sometimes even then you can't hear all the words, which is my only complaint.)

Sometimes Dylan uses logic, and sometimes abandons it to leap from image to image so quickly that he's bound to leave you behind occasionally. But if you need the security of knowing exactly what's happening at any given moment, poetry should be avoided.

It's hard to quote him effectively. He takes his own tough words and re-moulds them like modelling clay, throwing enormous emphasis on unexpected words, always hitting the rhyme with all his strength.

I write about the power and wit of his words because his singing is secondary, the best possible way of delivering the goods, and because his tunes are less startling and original than his lyrics.

Blonde On Blonde is mainly devoted to Dylan's wry study of himself and his women, but it varies incredibly in mood. *Rainy Day Women* is an outrageous National Anthem for the beats. *Leopard-skin Pill-Box Hat* is a wonderful assault on a sophisticated lady.

Sad-Eyed Lady of the Lowlands meanders soulfully for the whole of one L.P. side. *Obviously Five Believers* is happily swinging nonsense. *Fourth Time Around* makes witty, drunken use of the 'Norwegian Wood' theme. *Stuck Inside of Mobile* and *Visions of Johanna* show Dylan's surrealism riding high.

Influences? It's a waste of time comparing him with smaller talents. You could be listening to him instead, learning from this poet, this genius.[1]

---

[1] *Blonde on Blonde* reviewed by Adrian Mitchell, in *Woman's Mirror*.

7 Conclusion*

Fashion furnishes a departure . . . which is always looked upon as proper. No matter how extravagant the form or appearance . . . as long as it is fashionable it is protected against those painful reflections which the individual otherwise experiences when he becomes the object of attention. All concerted actions are characterized by the loss of this feeling of shame.[1]

The sociologist, Georg Simmel, wrote this piece about clothes fashions at the turn of the century, but he could equally well have been describing the pop scene in the 'sixties. Fashion, whether in music, clothes or dance, provides the young with a route to distinctiveness, originality and marginal rebellion which by-passed the insecurity and isolation felt by the lone wolf.

So the teenager may go to a modish West End club that is disapproved of by his parents, raided by the police, and ignored by the bulk of young people, but which is frequented by enough of his own kind to reassure him that he is not a freak but a trend-setter. A girl may wear a skirt of a highly original, personal design—but its hem will not be four inches below the knee if fashion is four inches above. The pop world is, in the strict sense of the word, a competition: its members are out to win but not to break the rules. A singer rarely attempts to be completely original, but merely to be successful or interesting within the framework of a fashionable trend. And even the most outlandish mod, in his restless search for newer and more

* February 1966.
[1] *International Quarterly*, Vol. X, 1904.

distinctive symbols of group differentiation, would not create a
new style for himself if he was not reasonably sure that some
others would follow him.

The mod cult which we examined in an earlier chapter can
perhaps give a clue to the role that fashion plays in the pop
scene. Although it is difficult to generalize about mods' backgrounds (I have known mods and rockers come from the same
family) they do seem to predominate amongst socially mobile
groups. On numbers in the streets at least, it is in the New
Towns and housing estates that you will find them, in Croydon
and Islington and Stevenage.

For young people in this sort of social milieu the pop scene
provides a welcome socializing influence. The music is exciting
and distracting, and provides a common language of shared
emotions. The camaraderie of the dance-hall and the reassuring
knowledge that the girl next door likes the same records are
community bonds, of a sort. And the whole atmosphere of the
pop world supplies a glamour and variety that is often conspicuously absent from the teenager's home and working life.
I don't think it's without significance that in 1963, when beat
music was at its zenith on Merseyside and overall juvenile
crime figures were up by nearly 10 per cent, those in Liverpool
were down by 2 per cent.

But it would be wrong to explain away the pop scene as a
giant social therapy institution. Although the obsessive concern
with fashion is most noticeable amongst the educationally
underprivileged, who have not perhaps been given the opportunity to express themselves in more substantial ways, there
are signs that this is changing. Most universities now have their
own rhythm and blues groups, where they once had jazz bands
that were right outside the pop sphere. More and more middle-
class thirty-year-olds are appearing amongst the club audiences.
In clothes, particularly, all the barriers are down, and the only
qualification now for shopping in Carnaby Street is the right
shape.

Perhaps the extension of pop's audience results from the fact
that it can provide two sorts of experience that aren't easy to
find elsewhere. The first is light-hearted and probably harm-

less: the opportunity for the silly adulation of favourite singers, for the performance of bizarre but exhilarating dances, for nostalgia, change and innovation. The second is the opportunity for some sort of total musical experience. In many ways, popular music today lies close to the primitive conception of music as a communal, functional activity. The idea of simply *listening* to music is comparatively new. Previously the audience was involved both physically and mentally in dancing and acting out social rituals to the rhythms.

At once we were plucked into a whirligig and cacaphony of vivid movement and hallucinating sound (heavens, those drummers!)—introduced to us by four spirit devils of the Mende tribe, Messrs Gorboi, Kongoli, Bundu and Nafali, all invisible beneath masks and costumes at once terrifying and tremendously reassuring by their verve, gusto and calculated abandon. What style, yet what wildness, this whole Sierra Leonean performance had! And how one envied the prodigious dexterity of Musa Kenema, the solo acrobat and contortionist, who flipped around the arena like a human helicopter! And how beautifully song, percussion and dancing, and men, women and children, moved and filled out the vast space with a sense of abundant life and mystery which could remind us that 'primitive' cultures are in fact so sophisticated, yet close to realities which we . . . have so largely lost.[1]

At a much less rich level, this is precisely the sort of communication that can occur at a live session with a group like the Animals. Eric Burdon's bitter face and voice, the sheer blistering volume of the music, the colour and movement of the dancers, all convey a very tangible emotional experience of what it means to be young—and how much these people dread the thought of being old.

There is, I believe, a place for both these sorts of experience in a popular music. The sad thing about the contemporary pop scene is that it provides on its credit sheet precious little else. There seems to be almost a barrier against music that expresses more subtle emotions, songs that express opinions and ideas. But as I hope may have become clearer from this book, this

[1] Colin MacInnes describing the 1965 Commonwealth Festival Great Dance Gala in the Albert Hall. *New Society*, 30 September, 1965.

seems to be more a result of the built-in conventions of the pop world than of a campaign of strategic manipulation by adults who are aware that too great a movement towards discrimination and complexity in pop music could spell their commercial ruin.

At every stage in the evolution of a pop song these conventions are at work, helping to determine not only the success of the song, but the very way it communicates. The writer who first conceives the song will have absorbed so much of the style current whilst he is composing that he will find difficulty in escaping its influence. He may even ape it deliberately. Moreover, to meet the functional demands made upon pop, the song's verses must be short, and its tune easy to remember. If it is a beat number it will be more successful if it is capable of being imitated by the thousands of local groups who play this music in dance halls.

As soon as the song is made public it will run the risk of being categorized with others with which it has no more than the slightest superficial connection. If it is plugged too much it may be killed by sheer over-exposure. If it is plugged too little nobody may ever hear it. If it has something to say there is a possibility that this will be obscured by the attractiveness of the singer or the excitement of the backing. If it is positively 'controversial' it may be banned by the broadcasting companies or aggressively trivialized by the disc jockeys. If it survives this treatment it will attract, quite innocently, poor imitations into the Hit Parade. The singer may even become his own mimic as he aspires to repeat his earlier success.

The cumulative effect of all this is the consolidation of a sort of pop *geist*, that exaggerates the importance of change, activity and exposure, and persistently sabotages any growth towards thoughtfulness.

But in spite of these institutionalized obstacles, discrimination is growing amongst the audience (though much more slowly than the sudden bogus increase is sensibility which the protest craze seemed to indicate.) British rhythm and blues, whilst by no means a personal music, has become the corporate voice of the urban teenager. Groups like John Mayall's Bluesbreakers, the Cream, Manfred Mann, and Alex Harvey's Soul Band have created, by developing sheer musical talent without musical arrogance, what has eluded most jazzmen: a music that is as exciting to dance to as it is to listen to.

In music purely for listening, too, there is a slow but steady advance. Burt Bacharach and Lennon and MacCartney have shown that it is possible to create powerful ballads without resorting to the antique sentimentality of Ken Dodd and Julie Rogers. And folk-songwriters like Dylan and Dick Farina are showing how far lyrics can be developed to comment on the contemporary world whilst still retaining a pop song quality.

But we may have to wait until 1968 to see in which direction pop is likely to develop. There seems to be a five-or six-year cycle in the pop scene, exciting and original at the peaks, but dull and repetitive in between: the rock'n'roll and skiffle booms were at their height during 1957–58; then there was a lean period until 1963–64 when Merseybeat and rhythm and blues erupted. (Perhaps this corresponds to generations of young people: the under thirteens in 1957 were just too young to 'belong' to rock'n'roll, and it was precisely this age group that created the beat music revolution six years later.) Now, in the Hit Parade at least, there seems to be a tailing off again. Beat music has become stale and montonous, and ballads, though not especially numerous or successful in Hit Parade terms, have moved into the limelight.

There is one final development which it would be pleasant to see. Pop music at present is shot through with the values and needs of young people. If ever there was an art form which was exclusively of the young, by the young and for the young, it is this one. When the songs speak cogently, they speak of problems which are those of the young; when they do not, they need the choreography of young bodies to invest them with any meaning at all. Nor, perhaps, could it be otherwise: the tide-race of fashion, the careless transfers of loyalties are reflections of the febrile but fickle dynamics of adolescence itself.

But it seems, nevertheless, a shame that adults should have to diet on the same fare, or else fall back once more on Sandy MacPherson. Perhaps John Lennon, who will be twenty-seven (and thus very much over the pop hill) if the boom arrives on schedule, could make his obvious literary talents a little more evident in his songs, and begin a tradition of contemporary, adult, popular music. Then, at least, more oldsters could take pop seriously without the nagging guilt that they were betraying their generation.

Pop grows up and Lennon obliges: 1967

Up to the end of the two World Wars there was supposed to be a vast gap between the serious and the popular arts. Straight composers—Schoenberg, Bartok or Stravinsky—were preoccupied with personal consciousness and conscience, bearing the burden of guilt for us; the pop entertainers offered us escape, hedonism or dreamful nostalgia. With a few exceptions (Berlin, possibly Kern) the best pop compoesrs were the most sophisticated: through the unexpected harmony, rhythmic contraction or melodic ellipsis—a defensive irony, a recognition that the dream, if a human need, wasn't true.

Today, the gap seems to be closing: for pop music now shares with jazz and with avant-garde non-pop a desire to retreat from the harmonic consciousness of the West, returning to the most rudimentary rhythm and line. The music of Boulez and Cage on the one hand, the Beatles and Boy Dylan on the other, may seem vastly different; yet they have in common a distrust of individual expression and an attempt to return to magic, possibly as a substitute for belief. In the music of Cage there's little body rhythm left, whereas the Mersey beat may seem to have little else; both, however, by their complementary if opposite paths effect a dissolution of consciousness. The girls who faint at a Beatle performance have attained the nirvana that Tristan' was seeking. In dancing alone, not with partners, young people evade the togetherness of a love-relationship which, however joyful, must hurt; their lonesomeness merges into a corporate act, a sundering of identity. The music provides a substitute for security: a pretence that we, the young in an unstable world, can stand or dance on our own feet.

The origins of this music, significantly enough, were in the most primitive form of the country blues. The cry of a dispossessed, persecuted, black minority provided the impetus for the mass music of white young people in a mass civilization. The Beatles' early numbers, indeed, betray, in their instinctive pentatonicism and modality, many features in common with medieval music and with primitive folk cultures, and very little in common with the harmonic practice of the 18th century and after. Some of these songs have just been reissued on a retrospective L.P. called *Beatle Oldies* (P.M.C./P.C.S. 7016). *A Hard Day's Night*, for instance, has no conventional tonic-dominant modulations but a distinctively plagal, flat feeling, and is riddled with blue false-relations and with oscillations between the triads of the tonic and the flat seventh comparable with those in the keyboard music of Gibbons or Farnaby; while *She Loves You*, though sometimes harmonized as though it were in E flat, has a pentatonic-tending tune of which the tonic seems to be an aeolian C. That such archaism intrudes even into the work of a sophisticated pop composer like Burt Bacharach suggests that there may be a growing-together of pop culture with the folk-song revival movement: a hint that is reinforced by the phenomenal success of Bob Dylan. The words of his early songs were often of poetic intensity, resembling real ballad poetry, the nursery rune, and even, on occasions, the songs of Blake. Musically, they were even more basic than Beatle tunes.

At this stage it would probably be true to say that Dylan's words, since they carried a message and were sometimes poetry, mattered more than his tunes, whereas the Beatles' tunes were more inventive than their verses. Both, however, have shown a capacity to develop and in developing have approached nearer to one another. On the Beatles' last L.P., *Revolver* (P.M.C./P.C.S. 7009) the words are decidedly worth listening to and, especially in the satirical numbers (*Mr Taxman*, *Dr Roberts*), have obviously been influenced by Dylan. As this has happened, the primitive and non-western elements in their music have been emphasized, both in the melismatic, folk-like vocal techniques and in the electrophonically produced imitations of rural folk-instruments such as bagpipes, jew's-harp and mountain dulcimer. Even *Yellow Submarine* comes off, because its musical inferiority is part of its ironic effect, which is a deflation of the impulse to escape. Other ballads combine social criticism with compassion: consider the poignant effect of the echoed refrain in *Eleanor Rigby*, with its square, string accompaniment. Other songs use the dream motive positively, advising us to recharge our spiritual batteries for tomorrow. In encouraging us to turn off our minds, 'relax and float down-stream', the extraordinary *Tomorrow Never Knows* discovers a new sonorous experience in amalgamating avant-garde jazz (Mingus-like jungle noises), Cage-like electronics, folk pentatonicism, Indian sitars. The Beatles' new E.P. (Parlophone R5570) extends this surrealistic tendency: *Strawberry Fields Forever* seems to be a hallucinatory L.S.D. song, with magical instrumentation—if with a not quite top-notch Beatle tune; *Penny Lane* brilliantly recreates everyday life in a state between sleep and waking, mingling Beatle song with jazz trumpets and brass bands on the march in a manner that may have been prompted by the music of Charles Ives.

The Beatles' words have grown to match their music; complementarily, a deepening and ripening of the musical aspects of Dylan's talent began with *Mister Tambourine Man*, most memorably haunting of all modern pop songs, and probably the initial impulse to the vogue for the hallucinatory. It's by no means all vogue, however, for if it looks superficially like an escape-song (and is such in so far as a tambourine man is a dope pedlar) it's also a moving appeal for another kind of commitment. In Bob Dylan's new album, *Blonde on Blonde* (C.B.S. 66012), most of the songs have comparable surrealistic tendencies; indeed the words are often so ambiguous as to suggest Gertrude-Stein-like automatic writing. As poetry, this looks suspect, as Dylan's earlier narrative ballads didn't. Yet in combination with the music, the words weave their spell (and the phrase is pertinent in that the new pop is concerned more with incantation than with communication). *Sad-eyed Lady of the Lowlands* is an apparently corny 6/8 waltz that weirdly evokes mystery and, in its 17-minute duration, makes time stop; and the song proves that Dylan is justified in being contemptuous of those purists who yell 'Traitor' when he unequivocally takes over electrophonic equipment. If this isn't a modern folk song I don't know what is; and a modern folk singer who ignores the resources of technocracy denies, rather than corrupts, his heritage. If there are moments in Dylan's later work when one wonders if he isn't a bit phoney, one never suspects him of stupidity.

Dylan and the Beatles seem to me the supreme talents in pop music today, and they have created an environment in which interesting if less disturbing groups, such as The Beach Boys, can emerge.

Certainly the finest music of Dylan and the Beatles can take its place alongside the best of modern jazz and some of the near-best concert music; is this deeply significant, or does it merely mean that they've ceased to be pop and that, their youth ending, they'll cease to be myth heroes and will become intermittent and occasional 'artists'? These latest discs seem to make an obsessive appeal to the brighter young (for instance, my students). On the other hand, the Beatles *Revolver* disc was dismissed by a class in a large, industrially-centred school with the ominous words: 'Aw no, sir, we don't like that; it's all chinky.'[1]

The new Beatle L.P., *Sgt Pepper's Lonely Hearts Club Band* (P.M.C. 7027), continues the trend initiated in *Revolver* and *Penny Lane*; though it starts from the conventions of pop it becomes 'art'—and art of an increasingly subtle kind. For one thing, the beautifully produced disc isn't just a collection of numbers, but a whole of which the parts, if remarkably various, are related. This whole is about loneliness; and the period comedy of *Sgt Pepper's Lonely Hearts Club Band*, which begins as a hilarious evocation of old-style (Edwardian?) camaraderie, is gradually transformed as the 'lonely' elements are detached from the hearts, the club and the band—the things that make us simple, social creatures.

So it's natural that the 'public' band piece should be followed by a solo appeal for 'a little help from my friends'; by a portrait of a dream girl, *Lucy in the Sky with Diamonds*; by a somewhat wobbly hope that, 'since you've been mine', things, though bad, are getting better; by a song about fixing holes to keep out the cold rain; and by a number about a girl leaving home, revealing the gulf between the generations. The technical means explored in these songs often seem quite sophisticated: especially when the poetic imagery is close to recent Bob Dylan (*Lucy in the Sky*) and when electrophonic devices are used to comment half ironically on simple sentiments and situations. Irony, moreover, is usually present in the musical material itself: for instance, the suddenly brisk refrain in *Lucy*, the rhyming incantation in *A Little Help*, the soupy cello solo and simultaneously uncomprehending duologue in *She's Leaving Home*, with its funny yet touching use of falsetto. All this doesn't affect the innocence of the tunes; indeed, one might say that the record is moving as well as amusing precisely because the bits of tune, still rudimentarily diatonic or even pentatonic, seem the younger, the more vulnerable in a world to which the simple solidarities of good old *Sgt Pepper* no longer apply.

[1] Wilfred Mellers, 'Sixties' in *New Statesman*, 24 February, 1967.

The innocence survives when, on side 2, the Beatles plunge into deeper water. The first number, explicitly about 'the space between us all', is also, significantly, the Beatles' most explicit homage to Indian music. George Harrison's tune and singing remain rune-like, rudimentary, despite quasi-oriental glissandi; yet they generate instrumental playing on sitar and tabla of a strange beauty and even complexity. As with the earlier *Tomorrow Never Knows*, the Beatles' Indian exploration seems to induce rebirth, for the next three songs are unequivocally positive, even if satirical. *When I'm Sixty Four* brilliantly reinvokes the pop music of Dad's youth, yet the tune and the scoring (is it the Beatles' own?) are so fetching that one accepts the corny ragtime with delight; no doubt there's also a suggestion that our pop music, when we're 64, will sound no less old-hat. The witty raggy song about *Lovely Rita, Meter Maid* is also at once comic and compassionate; and leads into a *Good Morning* song, a merry paean of created nature wherein beating Beatles are joined by barking dogs, mewling cats, and screeching birds. 'I've got nothing to say but it's OK', so the morning is good indeed, and can carry us back to an apparently triumphant reprise of *Sgt Pepper's* social music, with additional exuberant trumpet fanfares, applause and laughter off, a la Stockhausen's Momente.

But the Beatles, despite their priceless simplicity, aren't as simple as all that. The triumph is equivocal, though not double-faced: for there's an epilogue, *A Day in the Life*, which returns us to the loneliness of the young heart. The phrase the song opens with is one of the most typical, and certainly most haunting, the Beatles have ever created: a tender slip of a tune that tells us how 'I read the news today, oh boy', and though some of it is funny, more of it gives me the creeps. The naïve phrase changes as the beat grows stronger, and the song turns hallucinatory, opposing the dream within the mind to the nightmare outside. The B.B.C.'s ban on the song seems stupid, since the original tune remains so innocent and the (electrophonic) trip is so disturbingly scary. It seems to me the best song on the disc; and, like most of them, it's at once ripely funny and deeply sad. It helps us to understand the young, and I think it helps the young to understand themselves. There's only one moment of uncertainty—the leery laugh at the end of *Within You Without You*. I don't know how to take this; and I suspect that the Beatles don't either.[1]

---

[1] Wilfred Mellers, 'Lonely Beat' in *New Statesman*, 2 June, 1967.

Further reading

I have deliberately avoided trying to arrange these books in separate groups, as the pop scene's amorphousness means that any comment can be legitimately classed in a number of different categories.

ALLSOP, KENNETH (1967) 'Pop Goes Young Woodley' in RICHARD MABEY (ed.) *Class*. Anthony Blond.
A shrewd piece on the erosion of class barriers in the pop scene, written in the author's usual electric spray-gun style.

BIRD, BRIAN (1958) *Skiffle*. Robert Hale.
Not a very thoughtful or far-seeing volume, and the smell of the camp fire is too prominent. But it is the only book on the craze.

BRAUN, MICHAEL (1964) *Love Me Do*. Penguin Books.
A straight journalistic account of a few days in the life of the Beatles. Contains a few useful insights into the Beatles as people and their fans as objects.

FERRIER, BOB (1964) *The Wonderful World of Cliff Richard*. Peter Davies.
A euphemistic biography.

GOODMAN, PETE (1964) *Our Own Story by the Rolling Stones*. Transworld Publications (Corgi).
A monosyllabic yet unpretentious account of the group's rise to fame.

HALL, STUART and WHANNEL, PADDY (1964) *The Popular Arts*. Hutchinson Educational.
Chapter 10, 'The Young Audience', contains a thoughtful and

sympathetic analysis of the commercial, social and cultural significance of pop.

HECHINGER, GRACE and FRED (1964) *Teenage Tyranny*. Duckworth.
An unnerving account of the cult of adolescence in the U.S.A. Written from a shocked puritan standpoint, but facts are facts. Contains a chapter on pop idols and the rise of the Twist.

HUGHES, DONALD (1964) 'Recorded Music' in *Discrimination and Popular Culture*. Penguin Books.
An intelligent little essay which takes a synoptic look at the history and current musical status of jazz, pop and folk music.

JONES, LEROI (1963) *Blues People*. William Morrow.
A rogue of a book, inconsistent and sloppy in places, but basically a brilliant analysis of the meaning of contemporary negro music, written from the inside.

KEIL, CHARLES (1966) *Urban Blues*. University of Chicago Press.
Far and away the finest book yet written on popular music. The book ostensibly confines itself to contemporary American urban blues, but the author, an anthropologist, offers interpretations of such things as the dynamics of a pop concert, the symbolic status of idols, the kinesics of dance movements, that have a significance for all pop music.

KENNEDY, JOHN (1959) *Tommy Steele*. Souvenir Press.
Frank stuff about the promotional manoeuvres that lay behind the Bermondsey Boy's success, written by his manager.

LAURIE, PETER (1965) *Teenage Revolution*. Anthony Blond.
Perhaps the most intelligent book of all on British teenagers. Chapters 3 to 6 cover fashion, pop song lyrics, and 'some of the workings of the music business'.

LESLIE, PETER (1965) *Fab; the Anatomy of a Phenomenon* MacGibbon and Kee.
A tedious, clever-clever book about the British scene. The author worked as a publicist for a record company, and the book reads very much like an extended sleeve note.

MACINNES, COLIN (1959) *Absolute Beginners*. MacGibbon and Kee (Penguin edition 1964).
Still the best fictional coverage of the pop scene, in spite of the

fact that this is not its central theme, and infinitely better than books like Nik Cohn's *I Am Still the Greatest Says Johnny Angelo* and Thom Keyes' *One Night Stand* which do take it as their theme.

MACINNES, COLIN (1961) *England, Half English.* MacGibbon and Kee (Penguin edition 1966).
Contains wise and sympathetic essays on Tommy Steele and 'Pop Songs and Teenagers' that are amongst the first serious critical looks at British pop.

MELLERS, WILFRID (1964) *Music In A New Found Land.* Barrie and Rockliff.
A sparklingly written and monumentally intelligent book about the American musical tradition, relating classics to blues to jazz to pop.

NEWTON, FRANCIS (1959) *The Jazz Scene.* MacGibbon and Kee. (Penguin edition 1961.)
Contains some useful references to the relationship between jazz and pop.

OLIVER, PAUL (1960) *Blues Fell This Morning.* Cassell.
A fascinating and exhaustive analysis of the roots of blues lyrics in the negro's experience. A social history of coloured America in its own right.

OLIVER, PAUL (1964) *Conversations With The Blues.* Cassell.
Interviews with blues singers by the same author.

RIBAKOVE, SY and BARBARA (1966) *Folk-Rock: the Bob Dylan Story.* Dell.
A surprisingly sensible pulp paperback about the man, the writer and the performer. Contains a perceptive analysis of all Dylan's L.P.'s up to 1966.

SANDFORD, JEREMY (1967) *Synthetic Fun.* Penguin Books.
Worth reading to see just how prejudiced attacks on pop can be. Chapter 8 is almost a caricature of the 'hysterical moron' view of the teenage pop audience. Which is a sad thing to say about a writer usually so sensitive.

TUCKER, NICHOLAS (1966) *Understanding the Mass Media* Cambridge University Press.
This book, subtitled 'a practical approach for teaching' contains

a section at the end on pop. It doesn't come anywhere near under-standing the way pop works, but gives a few useful hints about how to handle it in the classroom.

WILSON, JANE (1967) 'Teenagers' in *Len Deighton's London Dossier*. Penguin Books.
A tiringly zippy but fairly accurate account of the London club scene circa 1966.